ADVERSITOLOGY

Overcoming
Adversity
When
You're
Hanging on
By a
Thread

Also by Frank McKinney

Aspire! How to Create Your Own Reality and Alter Your DNA

The Other Thief

The Tap

Dead Fred, Flying Lunchboxes, and the Good Luck Circle

Burst This! Frank McKinney's Bubble-Proof Real Estate Strategies

Frank McKinney's Maverick Approach to Real Estate Success: How You Can Go from a $50,000 Fixer-Upper to a $100 Million Mansion

Make It BIG! 49 Secrets for Building a Life of Extreme Success

FRANK McKINNEY

ADVERSITOLOGY

Overcoming Adversity When You're Hanging on By a Thread

Caring House BOOKS

FLORIDA

Dedicated to my friend Mike Magi,
who passed away from an adversity similar to mine.

This book is also dedicated to you, the reader.
After reading it you will have the tools and knowledge
necessary to overcome your adversity quicker
and with far less pain.

CONTENTS

INTRODUCTION

A-D-V-E-R-S-I-T-Y

WTF?!

On March 11, 2020, the entire world was thrown into chaos when the United Nations declared a global pandemic. Ironically, on this this very same day, Frank McKinney received an unrelated possible death sentence from his doctors . . .

In the weeks leading up to this, Frank is riding high. He has just celebrated the theatrical, rappelling-from-a-helicopter grand unveiling of one of the most beautiful oceanfront mansions in the world: his $15 million speculative "Tropical Modern" masterpiece at 3492 South Ocean in Palm Beach. After creating and selling 44 oceanfront mansions on spec, this magnum opus is now being marketed and billed as his final masterpiece. Frank thinks he is retiring after 30 years as the preeminent creator of beachfront mansions.

Now it's time to turn his attention back to the Mojave Desert and the footrace *National Geographic* has ranked the toughest one in the world: the Badwater 135-mile ultramarathon. As Frank contemplates returning to the searing heat of Death Valley, California, to compete for the 13th time at Badwater, he reflects on his faith and how many of the Bible's most significant and transformative events seem to occur in the desert. There's a deep spiritual cleansing that takes place there, a rawness and renewal unlike anywhere else on the planet. The trajectory of Frank's life has skyrocketed since 2005, the first time he ran this punishing race. Now he looks forward to putting himself to that physical, emotional, and spiritual test again—a microcosm of life—when he will run continuously over a span of 48 hours, much of it in 130-degree heat.

Frank will do anything to get back out to his summer desert home. Although he completed six races in a row in his early years with Badwater, more recently he finished only one out of the last six. On his latest attempt, he made it only 135 *feet* before freakishly tearing a tendon in his foot almost right after the starting gun sounded. He's getting older, but on this next attempt he's leaving nothing to chance. His diet is cleaner and more precisely calibrated than it ever has been before. He is also happy to be a living science experiment, a human Petri dish, when it comes to anything that will allow him to exceed the known limits of his body.

Which is why, on Valentine's Day in 2020, he undergoes a cutting-edge procedure on his ailing knees. His orthopedic surgeon extracts stem cells from deep within Frank's hip bone. Those cells are placed into a high-speed centrifuge and spun down to create a highly concentrated amount of white blood cells, which are then injected back into Frank's knees. In addition to cadaver cartilage implanted during a previous surgery, these "super cells" are intended to help regenerate disintegrated cartilage, brutalized from 40,000+ miles of running all over the world.

He is also happy to be a living science experiment, a human Petri dish, when it comes to anything that will allow him to exceed the known limits of his body.

All is well. The magic carpet ride that has been his life—though full of turbulence along the way—continues to fly at supersonic speed.

Coincidentally, Frank is scheduled for his semiannual physical only a week later. Being extremely fit, these regular doctor's office pilgrimages are more cause for medical wonderment than suspense or dread.

"You're one of the healthiest individuals I've ever had as a patient. Your vitals and bloodwork are like those of a 25-year-old!" Dr. Carol Huber often exclaims.

This visit is no different, except for one tiny thing. The bloodwork from the lab shows a slightly elevated white blood cell count. A higher level of WBCs is not uncommon in endurance athletes, though, due to their bodies being in a perpetual reparative state. More important, given the recent procedure that blasted a sky-high concentration of WBCs into Frank's system, this reading is of little concern.

"Come back in a few days and let's check it again to be sure. I'm certain everything is fine," the doctor says.

The second test shows the WBC count has jumped again, but not by much: from 12,200 to 19,500. (A healthy reading is anywhere between 4,000 and 10,000.) Still no cause for alarm. Frank, his primary care physician, and his orthopedic surgeon continue to attribute the rise to the aggressive and invasive procedure just two weeks before. Frank's body will process the excess white blood cells, they think, and all will soon return to normal. He certainly has no other symptoms. Frank is busy enduring 20-mile training runs and managing his real estate empire. They decide to test again in another few days.

Less than a week later, the levels soar to 99,000, and his doctor begins to doubt that such a precipitous rise is tied to some new-age stem cell procedure. Still, Frank doesn't worry; he had insisted that the orthopedic doctor extract as much stem cell material as he possibly could from his body, so this is just a side effect of his usual "if a little is good, a lot is better" approach to life. They schedule one more test a few days out.

Even though Frank feels no effects from the escalation in his white blood cell count, he thinks that it is time to do some research to find out what the hell might be going on: *When you stick your head in the sand, what sticks out of the ground? Your ass, to get kicked. What in the world could this be? Some terrible infection, a blood disease, or simply errors at the lab?*

There is also the unsettling fact that Mike Magi, one of Frank's closest friends, died only a few weeks before from a deadly blood disease. At the time, Frank was so distraught that he could not even attend the funeral and Nilsa, his wife, went in his stead. Frank had made an excuse and failed to show because he simply could not face it.

This is just a side effect of his usual "if a little is good, a lot is better" approach to life.

That afternoon, these worrisome thoughts are deeply buried when Frank is the center of attention during a glamorous photoshoot for *Boca Raton Magazine*. During the last shot at his seaside property, where Frank is sprawled across a couch on the rooftop lounge, his phone rings, and it's Dr. Carol. The photography team takes a break, and Frank gets up, walks to the railing, and looks out over the beautiful, azure-blue ocean some 45 feet below. He taps the little green phone icon.

The glamorous calm before the storm

Calmly but firmly Dr. Carol orders him, "Get Nilsa and head immediately to the emergency room. Your latest reading shot to over 200,000. I'll meet you there. You're very sick and could be dying."

For a guy who's made his living by adding zeros and multipliers to practically everything in his life, this is startling. Frank's reading is now 222,000 white blood cells per cubic milliliter, or over 40 times the normal range with no end in sight to the rapid increase. *What the fu*k . . . ?*

"You're very sick and could be dying."

Frank's mind is racing as he makes the 9-mile drive in his 1988 Yugo along the 35-mile-per-hour zone of Ocean Boulevard, a road he has driven countless times returning to his house from the sites of dozens of his oceanfront creations. He has also run thousands of training miles on this stretch over the last 30 years. As if in a trance, he stares through the car's windshield and grimly notes that his tiny Yugo is just about the size of a coffin. The familiar drive has turned into a torturously slow premortem funeral procession in Frank's swirling mind.

When Frank gets inside the door, he explodes into a towering rage. Screaming, throwing anything not nailed down, smashing glasses, tearing Bible pages, cursing God—this from a Christian. He temporarily loses it, while his wife, Nilsa, is simply terrified for Frank. Something is going on, and Frank is being *forced* into the hospital to find out what, exactly, it might be.

As if in a trance, he stares through the car's windshield and grimly notes that his tiny Yugo is just about the size of a coffin.

What he's not thinking about is how life in the VIP wing of Bethesda Hospital was actually pleasant. He had been admitted there previously when he had a portion of his large intestine removed due to sepsis, and he'd found his stay so pleasant, in fact, that he'd delayed checkout until after dinner was served by the private chef.

But this time, he has no mental bandwidth for pleasantries. Same wing, same amazing care, same Frank. But, after several days of tests and waiting on pins and needles, the doctors, Nilsa, and Frank finally convene to hear the verdict.

Hospital Day 1: WTF?

The outlook is grim on this March day—for the whole world, really. And it's uniquely bad for Frank as his Midas touch, his Teflon reality, is destroyed in an instant with three words.

Chronic. Myeloid. Leukemia. (CML)

Frank sees the bleak path ahead all too clearly.

He does not want attention, prayer groups, prayer warriors, a hospital room decorated with balloons and get-well cards, and plasma donations from everybody he knows. When it comes to this, he chooses *not* to be a "put it out into the universe" kind of guy. He will do this his way.

I'm going to die some day, but it will not be today, and it will not be from this, he vows.

And the mindset shift is on.

* * *

It has now been three years since Frank's diagnosis, and, except for one small hiccup, he has been completely clear of any trace of the deadly intruder for over two years. He is back and better than ever. What approach did Frank take, and what mindset did he apply, to overcome this seemingly insurmountable obstacle? What other challenges and setbacks has he overcome in business, in relationships, in his spiritual life, that were just as threatening, and how did he approach these adversities? Why did Frank choose to keep his condition a secret from all but five people outside of his doctors? (Not even his family knew!)

Buckle up, settle in, absorb, and enjoy the 9-step A-D-V-E-R-S-I-T-Y plan Frank shares so you can overcome your life's adversities quicker and with far less pain.

And finally, *why* is this book written by me, Frank McKinney, in the third person?

The Adversitometer

10 – Breaks the Adversitometer

8 – Intense

6 – Moderate

4 – Very slight

2 – Barely worth registering

0 – Not worth registering

A quick assessment to gauge the emotional severity of the adversity you are currently facing, whether it's physical, relational, or financial: The Adversitometer is a simple tool to pull out of your pocket, purse, or from your memory and ask yourself, *Just how much adversity should this situation truly represent in my life?* You can go to Adversitology.com and print out your own Adversitometer.

1 ACCEPT

Yes, This *Is* Happening to You

Adversities come in many different forms and intensities. But here's the good news: You will experience only two types in your entire life, external (innocent) and self-inflicted (consequential). The question is how each of us will manage adversity—all the roadblocks big and small. More important, how will you?

Frank McKinney considers himself a pretty enlightened guy, certainly one with a demonstrably high ability to overcome adversity. But that was in his old life, the one before he heard those three life-threatening words. When he receives the official diagnosis, all that enlightenment flies (crashes) right out the unopened window, immediately.

On that life-altering day, Frank, Nilsa, and his doctors meet in a well-appointed conference room in the VIP wing of the hospital. They gather around a walnut table in solid armchairs, the Florida sun streaming through the window to warm Frank's pensive face. The doctors take care to keep the mood upbeat after breaking the news. A plan is in place: Frank will be discharged and take medicine called Gleevec, an extremely potent chemotherapy in pill form. Already Frank's mind is racing ahead.

"So pills, then. I'll take them for 30 days, and then I'll be better . . ."

Of course, his doctors make no promises, but they don't kill his hope.

FRANK'S JOURNAL

Yes, there is a part of me that is scared, terrified. Yet there is a part of me that is really believing in good news. The best news that I could hear would be that I'm going to be OK. That I will get to continue living my life just as I want to. Dear Lord, will you bless me with that news today? I pray a simple prayer of thanksgiving for what you have done for me in my life. I pray that I am healthy, and that my white blood cell count returns to normal.

Protect my heart and mind from total collapse and, most important, protect my family.

I believe this will happen and that this health scare will help me put into perspective my priorities in life, which draw me closer to you and away from sin. Do you know the relief I will feel when I am told the good news? I want my heart to overflow with joy, Lord. I am praising you for blessing me, and in the event I don't hear the news I'm praying for, protect my heart and mind from total collapse and, most important, protect my family.

Walking out of the hospital Frank is still feeling and looking surprisingly good. There is some pain from the buildup of pressure inside his bone marrow, but for a man facing what could be a death sentence, he's doing remarkably well. As an endurance athlete, his mental and physical threshold for pain is much higher than average, and he knows how to manage it. *Home, pills, recover, great. This will be easily doable.*

Early the next morning he starts taking the medicine. Within 48 hours Frank is a wreck and on an extreme downhill trajectory. Never would he have believed his runner's body could disintegrate so fast.

Day four on the new regimen and Frank barely has the energy to get out of bed. Every cell in his body is crying out in excruciating pain. He is nauseous and throwing up for most of the day. Sweating profusely from raging fevers. At-home chemo is intensely painful, a war being waged on his body as the white blood cells die from the aggressive treatment attacking and killing them. He is subsisting on nothing but water, ice chips, and Pedialyte. It shows as 20 pounds vanish from his athletic frame during the first two weeks of this living hell.

He is subsisting on nothing but water, ice chips, and Pedialyte.

Nilsa must assist him to the bathroom (fortunately, it is not far, though it suddenly seems so). They perfect a maneuver they jokingly call the "choo-choo" where Frank stands behind his wife, drapes his hands over her shoulders, and they take halting baby steps for several minutes before arriving at the toilet that is only 30 feet from his bed. On a good day Nilsa stands 5'1", and that's with her hair teased high. A good foot taller (even on a really bad day), Frank looms over his wife and leans heavily upon her. These trips to the bathroom several times a day are all the activity he can handle, and when Frank is not throwing up, what is coming out of the other end is a bloody mess. He feels as though he is surely dying.

For those first two weeks Nilsa sleeps curled up in a little ball in the tiny, upholstered side chair at the foot of their bed. She wakes every half hour and peers over to confirm Frank's chest is still faintly rising and falling and her husband is still alive.

Frank being Frank, he had begun to create his own reality from the moment when they were sitting in the hospital conference room. The mental gyrations are the toughest. Completely aside from the grueling physical battle, Frank is grappling with the psychological torment of a man who had been in tip-top shape less than a month before and is now literally disintegrating. Only time will tell if the medication is effective, and if not, well, let the funeral preparations begin. Frank is suffering. He still cannot quite believe what is happening, and he pings back and forth between anger and disbelief. This is all too fast, too soon.

Nilsa sleeps curled up in a little ball in the tiny, upholstered side chair at the foot of their bed.

Everyone in Frank's wide circle has always been drawn to Nilsa, who remains somewhat of an enigma to fans and acquaintances. She is calm where Frank is often overly animated, quiet and retiring whereas Frank has been known to say, "If all the world's a stage, then I want a brighter spotlight." At public events where she sometimes (rarely) speaks, the entire crowd signs up to hear her. Speaking out publicly is simply not her nature, but when she does, it's always worth hearing.

NILSA'S STORY

Very few people know me well. Many know about my life with Frank but certainly not how I feel inside. Being married to Frank is a cross between a roller coaster ride and having a seat on a SpaceX rocket, but I am no easy pill to swallow myself. I am as stubborn as they come. When I set my mind to something, it's set in stone.

When we heard my husband's diagnosis, I knew quite well what was ahead of us. Our close friend Mike Magi had just died after being diagnosed with a similar condition, and I had spent a great deal of time at the hospital with his wife. This foe was a killer, and I was determined it wasn't going to take my husband.

Over the three decades that I've been with Frank, we've shared 10 lifetimes of experiences—extreme highs, debilitating lows, so many joys and sorrows. We've both played so many roles. And this time I needed to step up to be nurse, caregiver, aide, confidante—but above all, I was Frank's wife, a wife who was going to see my husband back to health. The love of my life was not going to die on my watch. That simply wasn't an option.

The love of my life was not going to die on my watch.

For two weeks Frank's fever was over 102 degrees, spiking higher every couple of hours. The weight simply melted off him. He could not tolerate food, and he was as weak as a kitten. Every hour I would ice down his entire body just to keep from racing him to the emergency room. In these early days of the pandemic I was afraid of the ER and the threat of contamination there. I also knew that in the hospital they would separate us, and I was unwilling to leave his side.

In that sense, however, the timing was divine. The entire world had stopped so nothing was expected of Frank. We were holed up inside our house like everybody else. But we were in the fight of our lives, separated from each other except when I was taking care of him. Frank was in our bedroom by himself most of the time, just listening to the air conditioner click on and off, contemplating his life and possible death.

FRANK'S JOURNAL

Yes, I have a serious disease that involves cancer of my blood. Right now the symptoms don't allow me to do anything. I am bedridden and barely have enough energy to hold this pen, but I'm compelled to do it, no matter how long it takes me to write this. My subconscious mind is screaming at me to get this down.

I really can't believe this has happened to me. Someone who was so healthy and able to do anything he put his mind to. Now what? What will be left of my hopes and dreams? My aspirations to author more books, run more Badwaters, and maybe even create more real estate artistry? What will become of the infectious energy I radiate to everyone I encounter?

What will be left of my hopes and dreams?

I wonder, who will this new Frank be? What will he look like? How long will he even be around? First, I will make it a point never to say or write the "CML" or "C" words again. I will have to be on medication until the composition of my blood corrects. I will keep this to myself and pray to God as I always have that he will help me.

————◈————

The lowest point for Frank is coming to terms with the realization that he must accept that he is going to die. Or not die. Somehow, he still cannot quite believe that this has happened to him. His mood swings wildly back and forth between a place familiar to him, optimism, and a complete stranger, despair. It's panic time, and Frank is all over his rosary and Bible, calling down every saint in heaven to help him.

There is a bit of irony in the fact that Frank has recently written a book with the subtitle *How to Create Your Own Reality and Alter Your DNA*. Not only has the DNA in his blood been altered, but his mind simply refuses to accept his new reality.

* * *

The rational mind dissolves, disintegrates, disappears when confronted with severe adversity. This is what is known as denial, the mind's way of protecting itself from an uncomfortable or threatening situation. When faced with the worst, the human brain is simply not capable of processing devastating news right away.

Denialism—the practice of denying what's true—is what's going on when someone is confronted with unbelievably shocking news and the very first word that comes out of their mouth is a simple, involuntary, and emphatic *no!* The mind races to protect itself from pain, in this case by denying *it* ever happened—*it* being a death, a diagnosis, a firing, a bankruptcy, a breakup. Denial is a powerful force that will help you through the reaction that follows devastating news. A cushion for the mind, a force field imbedded into our DNA and designed to keep the shock from penetrating our very being. In the initial stages of facing adversity, denial is unavoidable and invaluable.

Every single person has their own level of resiliency. Setbacks that would flatten most people roll right off the backs of others. Many people experience an abusive relationship or a painful, unwanted divorce or breakup and sink into despair for years (or forever). They are lost in a perpetual state of bitterness, regret, and recriminations, while many others go on to remarry, finding their happily ever after. Someone who filed for bankruptcy five years ago may now be a millionaire again, while someone else lost $25,000 on a deal and is afraid to get back into the game.

In the initial stages of facing adversity, denial is unavoidable and invaluable.

Whatever might be facing you, denial is more than understandable. But the real question is this: What is stopping you from moving on?

Why can't I process this? What's wrong with me? I'm getting divorced, losing my business, enduring a terrible illness—but I can't accept this?! There's a good reason: your mind is trying to protect you. Learn how to recognize this excellent defense mechanism and you will get to acceptance far quicker. Because being stuck in denial—really, being stuck in any stagnant mindset—is never a long-term solution.

We all know someone who lives in denial, the classic case being someone with a drinking or drug problem who refuses to listen to well-meaning words from concerned family and friends. They absolutely insist there is no problem, they can handle it, not a big deal, everything's under control. To admit and accept they might have a problem is too much to face. They are simply not ready to quit the marriage, the pills, the bottle. This can go on for years, for a lifetime. Don't let it be you.

THE ADVERSITOLOGY QUOTIENT

Every person on this earth, regardless of the length or circumstances of their life, faces an equal amount of adversity. In other words, the adversity one person experiences (or has experienced in the past) is no more severe or debilitating than anyone else's. Let's call this the *adversitology quotient:* In this human race, we're all on equal footing.

Controversial? Absolutely, especially when you consider such tragedies as a child with terminal cancer. What about the parents who are faced with the murder of their child? What about survivors of war, rape, and so on? Surely these people have faced far more serious adversity and heartbreak than the average person.

> **Let's call this the *adversitology quotient:*
> In this human race,
> we're all on equal footing.**

While there are certainly numerous adversities that blow past 10 on the Adversitometer and shatter it to pieces, in the end, the amount of adversity we all experience equals out. Some experience a blast of adversity in the form of a graphic tragedy only to move to acceptance, peace, and serenity far faster than those who haven't experienced the same can comprehend. It only seems like their trauma was worse than anything we can conceive. Or there are those who never experience "the big one," yet their adversities seem to trickle on and on for their entire lives. In the end, who has it worse?

Does the subjective definition of "worse" even matter? Not really. Only what we do to make it better for us and humanity matters. And here is the fascinating, even uplifting part about facing undeniable tragedy: Some who experience catastrophic adversity manage to turn it around and use it for good. These heroic people help others *not* experience the same pain, or at least minimize the adverse effects and tenure of an adversity in another. By lessening another's adversity we lessen our own, even retroactively, and in the end, the adversitology quotient is proven true.

Let's take the example of television personality John Walsh, whose six-year-old son, Adam, was abducted from a South Florida mall and murdered in the 1980s. For more than 25 years the family grieved while the crime went unsolved. But over that period John Walsh became one of the nation's most outspoken victims' advocates, standing up for parents in similar situations and empathizing with them as only he and his wife could. More important, the work featured on his show *America's Most Wanted* prevented countless future tragedies. By his actions, Walsh managed to soften the blow of the day he lost his precious child. Mercy seems to spread across those who use their adversities to lessen another's.

One might say, "That's all fine and good, but what if my neighbor's kid got run over by a bus?" In the case of at least one family, this actually happened. A decade later, the impact this child's mother has had—by creating rear bumper beepers for buses and campaigning to put new driving laws in place—has been simply amazing. So many good works from one mother who managed to channel her pain into activism since that terrible time. Her purpose, to use her own adversity to help others, has ensured the safety of so many other children.

Mercy seems to spread across those who use their adversities to lessen another's.

The good that can arise from adversity need not be so public. Every single day people choose to do good despite their personal pain. They write a blog post about their obscure condition and help others who live thousands of miles away. They write books about how they overcame grief, illness, and every kind of adversity to comfort others. They shine a light on such previously shameful topics as addiction or mental illness or homelessness to promote awareness and show the world we can persevere by applying empathetic action. These are truly cosmic gifts many give to the universe, and the universe (God) always reciprocates. No one escapes life without suffering. Why not choose to use your adversity for the good of others?

THE REASON WHY?

When hit with unwelcome news, most people tend to do tons of research to learn more about what is facing them and gain helpful information from others who have endured a comparable situation. But when there are too many "possibles" to predict any outcome, too much information is not necessarily a helpful thing. Part of acceptance is: Don't over-analyze, over-Google, over-educate yourself. Gain the knowledge necessary to come to terms with what you are facing, then accept it.

There is certainly a time to wallow and ponder and wonder and lament; everyone needs that time, and the mind demands answers. *How and why did this terrible thing happen to me?* The brain relentlessly goes over and over every possible clue, trying to pinpoint the crucial turning point. *If I hadn't driven home on that road . . . If I hadn't worked late all those nights . . . If I had quit smoking earlier . . .* If, if, if.

* * *

The mind races for an explanation, and Frank is no exception. Over the years, several people in Frank's circle have weighed in on his punishing running regimen. More than one person has mentioned that his yearly 135-mile run through Death Valley and the thousands of training miles pounding the hard pavement in the hot sun may not be the ideal lifestyle choice. And just for discussion's sake, how about that monomaniacal focus over a 30-year span on creating and selling mega-mansions on speculation? Focusing on the minutest details, down to folding the toilet paper in each of his bathrooms to a perfect diamond-tip point? And all the related stress, conscious and subconscious? Perhaps that was not entirely . . . healthy?

* * *

Throughout life you will experience only two types of adversity: external (innocent) and self-inflicted (consequential). The first, external, is the type of adversity brought about from an outside force or occurrence. You are entirely innocent. Your child becomes gravely ill. You are in a terrible car accident because of a drunk driver. The stock or real estate market crashes. Your spouse or significant other decides to join the monastery or convent. It's September 11, 2001, and you're getting on a plane to San Francisco or headed into the office in the World Trade Center for another day of work.

> **Throughout life you will experience only two types of adversity: external (innocent) and self-inflicted (consequential).**

However, if we're going to get real here, much of the adversity we face is not due to external circumstances. It is the absolute opposite: It's self-inflicted harm that results in consequences in the form of severe adversity. In many of these cases, it's all (or at least a good part) on you. You took too much risk, didn't understand your market, and were forced to file bankruptcy. You cheated on your spouse, got caught, and they divorced you. You smoked or drank for decades and got sick. It's not the universe or other people doing you wrong, and you'd better accept that.

Self-examination is an exceptionally good thing, yet many people will go to great lengths in life to avoid such introspection. Self-reflection is important for the simple reason that it leads to truth. In fact, as the great philosopher Socrates said at his trial, the unexamined life is not worth living. We often spend a great deal of time avoiding truths in life (denialism) by any means possible. Overworking and self-soothing with drugs or alcohol or food or shopping are some of the most common. Escaping and seeking comfort seems easier than facing the truth. But it's not.

* * *

Is Frank's adversity external (innocent) or self-inflicted (consequential)? Either way, the experience is one hell of a baseball bat smack to the head.

So Frank dives deeply into this soul-searching examination. During the first two weeks of his illness he is forced to wonder if this just might be God's way of getting his attention. There was a time not long ago when Frank's life was very much out of control. He had been flirting with disaster—again. Taking risks by dancing on the razor's edge—again. Coming close to destroying not only his family but himself—again.

He believes that every now and then, when people simply will not listen, God reaches out and knocks them upside the head. Is that what's happening here? "Hey, Mr. Midas, Mr. Teflon Reality, you're dancing awfully close to disaster—again." *Bam!*

Frank most certainly had not been living up to his best self in the years just before this diagnosis. Could it be payback from the universe, karma, something like that?

"Oh, by the way, I'm doing this because you are too important to me, and I love you."

Maybe God himself was saying, "Enough, Frank! I've given you so many breaks already . . . this time, I'm going to really get your attention. This time, you're not even going to be physically able to leave your house. And oh, by the way, I'm doing this because you are too important to me, and I love you."

* * *

So the worst has happened. It's been building for a long time, or it's a bolt out of the blue. You may think, *Not me, my marriage is great.* Then next week your spouse runs off with a neighbor. Or, *My business is doing fantastic,* and in six months it's bankrupt. *My heath is perfect,* then out of nowhere the doctor at your routine boring physical says you're dying. The rational mind will deny it at first then search for answers. But the day comes when it's time to face it. It happened. Stop whining on social media. Stop whining at all.

Accept it and move on. But how?

* * *

After two weeks of being confined by his condition, Frank decides it is time to try activities he enjoyed before adversity struck. Things that brought him joy, got him out of bed every morning. He knows that choosing to relentlessly move forward is a major turning point in acceptance: trying to slowly trickle back in some of those activities that are fun, familiar, life-affirming, and, for Frank, perhaps life-saving.

That means he wants to get outside again, and Ocean Boulevard (State Road A1A) is his training ground. So Frank makes a decision: He will leave the house for the first time (apart from visits to the doctor in a wheelchair) and go somewhere under his own power.

FRANK'S JOURNAL

Sure, there are times that I'm angry, but what good does that do? I will fight. I need something to fight towards. I would love to return to Badwater, and I have an entire year to get ready. It is still a possibility. I likely won't be healed by that time. First and foremost is letting go of any blame, anger, or resentment and accepting what is.

ILSA'S STORY

One day Frank looked at me and said, "I want to go across the street." Meaning: walk across A1A, which is all that separates our house from the beach. I nearly went into coronary arrest. Still, I know Frank. Inside and out. What makes him tick, what makes him happy. I knew that getting outdoors was one thing that would return some joy to his life, so I didn't bother to argue.

I just said, "Here we go." I certainly expected to accompany him on the entire journey, however long or short it might be.

We set out that night under cover of darkness. Frank was insistent that no one see him in his deteriorated condition.

Down the stairs we went, oh-so-slowly and carefully, with the familiar choo-choo maneuver. Through the front door, then some tricky negotiation down the wooden steps to the driveway. We shuffled off the last step, then he turned and looked at me, and did I ever know that look.

We set out that night under cover of darkness.

"I want to try," was all he said.

I knew what he meant. Inside, I cursed. "I'll follow you," I offered.

"No" was his response.

Dammit.

So I just stood there and held my breath as my husband stumbled down the driveway and toward the street. He stopped at the edge of the road, and I could see Frank studying this familiar, nearly flat surface like it was a small mountain. I raced back inside the house and ran upstairs to our second-floor balcony, where I had a clear view of him. He was moving at a turtle's pace, looking none too steady, agonizingly slow and wobbly, step by painful step, but he was moving completely under his own power. It was what he needed, and I knew it, but it was torture to watch. Picture a 90-year-old man who forgot his cane and suddenly finds himself in the middle of the grocery store parking lot, with no help, trying to find his car. That was him.

He made excruciatingly slow progress. I was waiting for the moment he would fall and land in the bushes or, worse, on the pavement. Then what would I do? *He hasn't eaten for a week* was all I could think. *He is going to keel over!* He was so skinny and fragile. This was terrifying for me to witness. He quit moving for a few seconds, unable to take another step, and my heart stopped once again. But Frank somehow got himself across the street. I could not believe my eyes.

Frank glanced up, saw me on the balcony, looked me in the eye and began to sway and wobble again. I was sure he was going down, but he managed to catch and steady himself. He then sat down on the retaining wall and waved at me. My heart slowed down. *I will stand here and watch. This is something he needs to do,* I told myself.

Picture a 90-year-old man who forgot his cane and suddenly finds himself in the middle of the grocery store parking lot, with no help, trying to find his car.

After 10 minutes of catching his breath, when I saw him painfully stand up and start to make his way back, I raced back outside to meet him at the edge of our driveway. We returned to the house together. This little jaunt was so exhausting for him that he was completely wiped out, but he was so filled with joy. Now he had a glimmer of hope.

Frank's mind is the strongest thing he has. It is his mind that has brought him to where he is in his life. And in this slow procession across the street, he persevered. He did not give up. This caused me to become stronger. It was going to be quite the journey, and it started with those steps.

Prior to entering the house after his sojourn, Frank throws up in the bushes, but this doesn't dent his elation. He's made it! He then lies flat-out exhausted in bed for most of the rest of the night, but that doesn't stop him from putting his running clothes and shoes by the bathtub in preparation for the next day's workout, just as he's done thousands of times before training runs over 25+ years.

**A few years ago at the Badwater finish line—
and maybe someday again, but for now, one mile will do**

The next morning, Frank slips out of the house at 4:30 a.m. While Nilsa sleeps, he makes a journey of six entire blocks that takes him 33 minutes to traverse. This is the invalid's version of what Frank refers to as a "shock run" to expand the elasticity of his "no limits" mindset. There is certainly no actual running involved, but he's stretching the limits, for sure. On the third day, another real push, he doubles down once again, this time going an entire mile that takes 55 minutes. The confidence built from these training sessions or shock runs is intense but fleeting. Resuming an exercise routine, even one this simple, takes everything out of him.

One day he tells Nilsa, "I don't know if all this is worth it. I feel better sitting still."

Sitting still and refusing to accept is a death sentence.

Of course, he does. But that statement goes against everything Frank believes in. Sitting still and refusing to accept is a death sentence. We must take proactive measures to overcome any form of adversity. Wallowing is easy. Action is hard. *Never* sit still in your adversity. Accept it and face it down!

YOUR TURN: ACCEPT

- With an honest assessment, determine if your current adversity is, or your past adversities were, external (innocent) or self-inflicted (consequential).

- Where on the Adversitometer does your adversity fall? Hint: Most adversities aren't as bad as you think they are.

- Consider your internal dialogue. If it's taken on the form of denialism for an extended period, change the narrative.

- Accept it *now*. By doing so you'll begin to move past denial, blame, anger, and resentment.

Some of my past adversities are external:
- Growing up in the circumstances I did it was tough not having much.
- Learning to accept a dad who had substance abuse as well.
- Never growing up with my brother.

My internal adversities:
- Dealing with toxic women
- Dealing with multiple females
- Drug use
- Loosing my children to foster care.
- Not being in my older children's lives
- Not having a relationship with my mother.
-

2 DISIDENTIFY

Give It No Energy

By the end of this chapter, you will understand why this book is written by me, Frank McKinney, in the third person . . .

You give adversity as much power as you are using to wage war against it. When you renounce something, you're tied to it through the energy you use to fight it. Fight it and you empower it, period.

The trick is to disidentify. Similar to but far deeper and more elective than denial, disidentification is another protective mechanism of the mind. It's defined as removing a potentially harmful threat from one's self-identity as insulation from anxiety or failure. Taking this one step further, the *APA Dictionary of Psychology* notes that disidentification can be part of the meditation process, a benign separation from one's sense of self, a stepping-stone away from self-identity to attempt to observe oneself objectively.

When you renounce something, you're tied to it through the energy you use to fight it.

* * *

Frank, Nilsa, and their daughter, Laura, are about to learn all about the power of disidentifying.

For Frank, it's one of the hardest yet most enlightening lessons, one that has dawned only during this strange time while he is confined at home. And it runs entirely counter to his adrenaline-fueled life so far, a life with more than its share of business, personal, and physical challenges. Fight, flight, or freeze is the classic stress response, and Frank has always chosen to fight under fire. It goes back to his earliest childhood. It's encoded in his DNA. As an adult, whenever he has trained for and run ultramarathons, he has painted his face as an homage to his Native American battle spirit— because he knows he will have to rely on the warrior mindset to get him to the finish line.

But in this new situation, willpower and the warrior mindset are not enough, and they quickly prove to be a futile waste of Frank's precious energy.

* * *

The entire landscape is eerily deserted as lockdown regulations are in full force. COVID-19 has intruded on the entire world. Every television station posts rising death tolls on the nightly news, along with scenes of people dying outside packed hospitals; families stuck outside glass walls, unable to say good-bye to the stricken; and bodies stacked up in large, refrigerated tents outside morgues. Everyone is watching death come closer every day.

Frank finds this coverage oddly addicting, though these hours spent viewing are far from helpful. In fact, seeing this stuff only brings his mental state and spirits way down. He knows full well that when creating your own reality, those four ubiquitous screens—the phone, the tablet or laptop, and the television—serve to distract, counter, and even destroy the process of creating your own reality. Eventually, Frank shuts down all of them and chooses not to watch the coverage again. He refuses to allow this pandemic, over which he has zero control, to hamper his own recovery in any way.

Meanwhile, he is reestablishing his routine, starting with the tradition of laying out his workout clothes and shoes each night. Early each morning,

Frank dresses entirely in black, including hat and large mask, to disguise himself before he heads out to shuffle along Ocean Boulevard. He would be the first to admit his vanity—how the hair, the clothing, the entire "look" he has carefully cultivated are a large part of his brand—and he wants to preserve that identity. He is extremely wary of being recognized in such a feeble condition, though there aren't a whole lot of people on the streets at 4 a.m.

> **The few people outside that morning see a skinny man wearing dark clothes struggling to extricate himself from the tangle of branches and leaves, and they probably assume he's just a drunk.**

The disguise serves another purpose, too. The newly imposed City of Delray Beach curfew doesn't end until 6 a.m., so he needs to be fully camouflaged. No need to get arrested on top of everything else.

Sure enough, one day as dawn is breaking, a police car slowly cruises toward him, and Frank dives into the bushes to hide. (Would they really have arrested him for breaking COVID curfew? Doubtful, but Frank makes it a game to engage his mind as he struggles to break 3 mph on his 90-minute outing.) Minutes later, the few people outside that morning see a skinny man wearing dark clothes struggling to extricate himself from the tangle of branches and leaves, and they probably assume he's just a drunk after a long night. His fellow curfew violators, most of them on bikes, give him a wide berth. This is more than fine with Frank, as he is afraid even to pass someone on the sidewalk who might be infected with COVID. His immune system is utterly compromised and he's completely vulnerable.

On top of his diagnosis, Frank is dealing with another problem resulting from the chemo medication: atrial fibrillation, an irregular and often fast heartbeat that results in lack of blood flow throughout the body. This A-fib is quite dangerous in his weakened condition, and feeling faint is a constant problem while exercising. Frank manages to work up to a steady speed of about 3 mph by walking 80 percent of the route and "running" the remaining 20 percent (which is hardly running at all).

Upon his return he enters his home sauna. In normal times, he would spend an hour in the sauna with the temperature at full blast, 170 degrees, and run on the treadmill he'd installed inside so that he could heat-train. That is out of the question at this point, but Frank turns on the treadmill anyway, and then sits on the wooden bench to watch it go while he rests. He bakes in the intense heat as the conveyor deck makes loop after loop, and he visualizes the day when his sweat-soaked shoes will be pounding away on that treadmill again, first walking then running. The sweat pours out of Frank's body as he downs a gallon of Evian and pictures the deadly intruder leaving his body through the tiny holes on his skin. Yes, every pore is an opportunity to expel the unwanted guest.

A long-time believer in the power of visualization to create one's own reality, Frank uses this time to foresee a healthy and happy future. An avid, near-daily journaler for decades, he has been too worn out from the side effects of the medication combined with his exercise regimen to even bother to pick up a pen, other than for one brief journal entry, for three entire weeks, probably the longest he's gone in his adult life without writing. Not to mention his mind is too frazzled to gather his thoughts and concentrate. But today he picks up his journal again.

FRANK'S JOURNAL

I pray for just "One Day." One perfect day. One day with no worry about whether I'll live or die. One day with good sleep. No lack of energy. No excruciating all-over body pain. No setbacks. No headache. No A-fib. No worry about my white or red blood cell count. No heartburn. No rash, no fever, no chills, no forcing myself to eat. No throwing up, no nausea. No checking my watch in the middle of the night. No anxiety, no fear.

A day full of smiles, laughter, joy, and dance. A day full of energy, enthusiasm, gratitude. A day where I exercise and feel great afterwards, like my old self. A day when I can run with strength in my legs. A day when I spring out of bed. A day when my eyes sparkle with life. A day of internal peace and contentment. A day Nilsa and I are happy and free from what causes us both stress and anxiety. A day when Nilsa gets good news that brings her joy, a day free from worry for my wife. Yes, this would be my One Day. Until that One Day comes, I will be happy with parts and pieces of my perfect One Day. As I experience a blessing of little single elements of my One Day, I will continue to give thanks to God. One Day of peace and love.

***

Life for people all over the world, not just for the three McKinneys, has shrunk down to the boundaries of wherever they call home. Fortunate for this little family, lockdown is not particularly rough, as they have a tropical jungle for a backyard, and trees more than 100 years old tower over the oceanfront estate with a main house, guest house, tree house, pool, gym, and sauna. It's spring in Florida, a beautiful time to be outdoors and enjoy all the comforts of their historic 1935 home.

Still, Nilsa is having a tough time. As the only person who goes out of the house on errands, when she returns, she sits outside, dressed in what looks like a hazmat suit, washing all the groceries, bags included, before bringing anything into the house. She is that concerned about outside germs contaminating her husband's weakened system.

She is also worried about their daughter, Laura, whose life has been completely upended. Laura should be finishing her senior year and her term as student body president of Penn State University. Instead, she is back with her mom and dad for the duration.

$\mathcal{L}$AURA'S STORY

I was on my last spring break, out every night dancing in South Beach with my friends, having the time of my life. We did not have a care in the world. Just as we were packing our suitcases and preparing to head back to class for our last three months, we all got e-mails or texts from our respective schools saying, "Don't come back to campus. Due to COVID, everything is shutting down . . . classes will be held remotely . . . and we apologize to the seniors."

Just before I'd left for spring break, Penn State had held its 47th "THON," an annual 48-hour dance-a-thon to raise money for cancer research and the support of patients and their families. I'd completed the two-day event and devoted my efforts to "Standing for Mike" in remembrance of my dad's friend who had recently passed away. I stayed on my feet for two days and nights in honor of Mike and his family, especially his daughter, who was a classmate of mine and simply devastated by this loss. I could not imagine her pain.

Not two weeks later, my on-campus college experience was over for good, and I was locked down at home with my own desperately ill father.

I'd had such big plans: Graduate from school then head to New York City, find my dream job, and start my dream life. None of that was going to happen now. It was time to put on my big-girl panties. I couldn't break down about my own troubles, and my parents had much bigger fish to fry. So instead I put on my blinders and concentrated on immediate goals. First: graduate. I had to come to terms with the fact that there would be no traditional graduation ceremony with me in cap and gown, strolling across the stage, my proud parents in the audience. There would be no apartment hunting in the Big Apple. My parents needed me, and I needed to take care of them as best as I could.

For the next few months, from March to May, I wanted to be a student first but ended up becoming a near-full-time spokesperson for the university. At the president of Penn State's personal request, I was creating speeches, press releases, and videos to help the 46,000 suddenly displaced and confused students. "I can't figure out online classes." "My Wi-Fi's not working." "Where do I go for healthcare now?" "I can't afford this." "I might have COVID." "How do I find a job in these conditions?" I received several hundred e-mails like this every day and tried my best to direct each one to the proper resources.

I wanted to help my school and fellow students. Meanwhile, the last of my finals were approaching, and if I didn't pass them, I would not graduate. These senior-level classes were no walk in the park, but schoolwork took a backseat to my other responsibilities at Penn State.

My dad's health struggle was on my mind 24 hours a day, and I was hesitant to get physically near him. None of us had any idea of what was going on with COVID, and I had just been around hundreds of people exposed to who-knows-what germs, so I kept my distance.

One day my mom was out at the grocery store and my dad needed help. I could hear him calling her name, forgetting she was not home. I put on a mask and gloves, and covered my clothes with a raincoat, not sure what would happen when I entered the bedroom. All he needed was for me to put a straw in his drink. That's how weak he was. I had never seen Dad so sick. He looked out of it and ravaged. It was a shock. I had not gotten this close to him while he'd been ill, and Dad has always been a larger-than-life figure. In this moment he was so small and frail and human. It was a real wake-up call to see him this way, and for the very first time, the unwelcome thought crept in: *I don't know if my superhero dad is going to make it.*

I immediately banished it, though, because in my deepest self I always knew he would be OK. Perhaps it's because I had seen my dad get through so many obstacles professionally and personally. I just knew he would also somehow make it through this. No, it wouldn't be easy, but I told myself every night when I lay in bed ready to sleep, *My dad is going to be OK. There's a lot going on right now, but I will pray for him, be there for him, and trust that he will be fine.*

I was already struggling with the abrupt changes in my own life. Now I was being pushed with such an insane level of stress that I had no choice but to disidentify. It happened very naturally for me. A part of my brain simply shut down and went into survival mode. *I must detach my emotions from this. I'll deal with all of that later. For now, I must put my head down and get through this.* So that is what I did.

In Frank's case, disidentification started with a vow never to say the name of his condition again. After the meeting in the hospital discussing the official treatment plan, he no longer permits his own doctors to say those words, either. He has warned all medical staff that he will blot out any health reports that include this term. Without even speaking about it, he and Nilsa have agreed on this from day one. Both decided, *No, we will not give this disease and diagnosis any of our power. It will not be a part of us.*

Frank calls it a condition. He calls it an intruder or an unwanted visitor, because he refuses to empower it by using its name and any subsequent definition tied to that name. His formula: no absorption of adversity! Frank decides, *I will not allow this intruder to ruin my life. I will not give it the power or license to do that. OK, Mr. Intruder. I choose not to renounce you, and instead I will understand you.*

He has warned all medical staff that he will blot out any health reports that include this term.

Laura goes along with this ban, too, without being asked.

And his old morning routine, albeit altered slightly, gets back on track. The progress is incremental, but it is coming. Frank is trying hard to trickle in those elements of his One Perfect Day, which always includes prayer, exercise, and going outside. For fear of being discovered, he is certainly not yet ready to leave the house and "run" after the sun has come up. Several weeks into the new regime, he is still struggling. So he sets up a course on his own property. With the built-in twists and turns, this distance from

The life-saving statue, one-tenth of a mile at a time

one end of the deck to the other is exactly one-tenth of a mile. A practicing Catholic, he touches a two-foot plaster statue of Mary each time he finishes a lap. Back and forth he goes, trying for a mile at least, just to keep hope alive.

It is an excellent time for meditation on the nature of disidentification, which is one of the hardest lessons he's ever grappled with. Frank is coming to understand that his negative feelings about the current adversity are present only inside of him, not anywhere else in the great big world or in any external reality. *This is happening to "me,"* he thinks, *but it's not happening to "I."* That distinction is a bit out there, but he has plenty of time to engage in deep thought about the nature of "I versus me" and the power of seeing through adversity as opposed to fighting it.

"I" VERSUS "ME"

You can change your hat or your hair color, but it doesn't change your thinking. You can change your pen, but it's not going to change your handwriting. You can switch political affiliations, you can even change your gender expression, but the "I" stays sacred and immutable. The "I" is the observer and is unaffected by watching "me." The "I" is the internal guide, the soul.

Some people adhere to a deceptively simple practice known as the Blue Sky theory. How, you might ask, does one become the Blue Sky? Imagine that your mind is a cloudless sky, and that life's joys and small pleasures are puffy white clouds and sunny days, while adversities are dark clouds. These ominous clouds darken the sky, hurl down thunder and lightning, cause destructive storms and chaos, frighten people. Yet even the biggest, darkest thunderclouds all pass. All clouds drift and disappear, even the pretty ones, as does adversity. By its very nature, adversity is fleeting (in the grand scheme of an entire life) and temporary. Even a terminal illness is temporary, as you will die soon enough, or you will recover.

> **Imagine that your mind is a cloudless sky,
> and that life's joys and small pleasures are
> puffy white clouds and sunny days,
> while adversities are dark clouds.**

What's so powerful about Blue Sky is that it prevents overidentifying with something that is ultimately impermanent. In other words, you don't diminish yourself by allowing passing experiences and circumstances to cloud your sense of the "I."

Taking nothing away from the millions of people who have gained their sobriety and even saved others' lives through Alcoholics Anonymous, their traditional greeting leaves a lot to be desired. "Hi, I'm ———————, and I'm an alcoholic" undermines the incredible change they have made or are making. (It's likely that people succeed with the program because of the 12 steps, not this apparent overidentification that can continue for an entire lifetime, even after decades of staying clear of any alcohol.)

If you overidentify with your demon, you give it power. Instead, see through it. Understand it and the true value you place on it. Renouncing bad habits is something people do, dramatically, every day. *I will never drink alcohol again. I will never do drugs (or smoke another cigarette, eat sugar, or gamble, or date my old girlfriend, and so on) again.* That's impressive and it's not easy to fulfill. That relies on willpower and not understanding.

The key is to shine a light on the "whys."

What's more, by renouncing something, you become tied to it forever, as with the AA greeting. The key is to shine a light on the "whys." Become aware of the reason you have allowed this into your life and, more important, how you have come to see it as some indomitable, uncontrollable force. Understand it, and the burden will drop from your hands. It is through understanding the obsession, and your dependency on it, that it slowly disappears.

* * *

Exactly one month plus one day after Frank's diagnosis, Easter morning arrives. On this day when Christians celebrate the defeat of death and hope for humankind's salvation, Frank wakes up feeling inspired. If Jesus rose on Easter, so will he! He is out the door for five miles well before dawn, and for the rest of the morning he pays the price. Frank, Nilsa, and Laura turn on the television to watch the mass being livestreamed from St. Patrick's Cathedral in New York City. Despite his best efforts, Frank nods off and misses seeing most of the beautiful service and elaborate flower arrangements.

Many nights Frank still struggles to stay upright to eat at the kitchen counter. He usually starts leaning involuntarily after just a few minutes, forces down whatever food he can, leaves his perch on the treacherous stool, and heads to the couch, where he lies alone and listens to his wife and daughter chat in the kitchen. Feet up, pillows propped behind him, blankets close, yet feeling envious of simple dinner conversation he can no longer be a part of. He hears every word, but he can't join in. By the end of the day, he doesn't have enough energy to sit up on his own.

Frank sees Laura early one morning as he is returning from his dawn shuffle. His daughter is also outside, in the backyard punching away in the near-dark at the heavy bag she uses for kickboxing. Both are momentarily startled.

"What are you doing up?" he asks her.

"What are you doing out, Dad?" Laura responds. "How far did you get today?"

"Oh, I couldn't make it that far today, honey. Only about two miles." They smile at each other and go their separate ways. Laura resumes pounding away as Frank heads to the sauna.

Each member of the McKinney family is fighting their own silent battles. None wants to burden the others with their troubles. They are a close, unified family unit, but each of them has the tendency to internalize their challenges and avoid putting the weight of worry on anyone else. All three are getting good at disidentifying with adversity: They keep their worries to themselves, refuse to give their energy to adversity, don't live in the past, and keep pressing forward.

The baby steps are paying off. The progress is incremental, but it is coming. Frank's numbers begin to drop fast. In just one month, Frank's white blood cell count goes from 250,000 (at its highest in the hospital) all the way back down into a normal range at 4,700. The harsh medicine is doing its job. It kills those white blood cells. But it also attacks other important and energy-giving essentials like hemoglobin, hematocrit, and platelets. The treatment for his condition is both a blessing and a (temporary) curse, neither of which has anything to do with Frank's "I."

$\mathcal{L}$AURA'S STORY

In terms of fulfilling my requirements to graduate, I cut it a little closer than I would have liked. It all came down to one exam that I managed to pass by three points. I squeaked by, but that was fine with me. The enormous weight that came off my shoulders once it was officially confirmed that I would graduate was a huge relief. I was also very much looking forward to wrapping up my position as president of the student body.

I did not leave our property for 48 straight days. I knew my parents were concerned about my complete lack of a social life. Although they weren't supposed to, plenty of teenagers and young adults were spending much of lockdown hanging out together. My dad completely understood this mindset and didn't blame them, as they were young, healthy, not worried about germs or a little cold and certainly not about COVID protocols. Dad kept urging me to go out and see some friends, but I would not have dreamed of endangering his health in that way. I did not set one foot past our driveway.

And then those small steps, like the thousands and thousands Dad took out on Ocean Boulevard and back and forth across our property, started to pay off. When Dad talked the doctors into allowing him to slightly ease off the medication that was killing his white and red blood cells, Mom and I began to notice a shift in his mood, vitality, and energy levels.

And then, online graduation day arrived!

The university livestreamed Penn State President Eric Barron's address along with some prerecorded segments of my speech and others from student government. I watched the ceremony on television with my parents from our couch, certainly not the stately occasion I had envisioned. Halfway through, I burst into tears from sheer amazement that I had made it to this moment, and the pure gratitude I felt that Dad was well enough to make it downstairs and sit next to me and share in this experience. Then I had a great surprise!

All my friends who lived locally showed up at our house for a party outdoors. I had not seen anybody since spring break for fear of germs. I could not have been more delighted to see them all and to realize that, despite what they were enduring, my parents had managed to arrange such a celebration for me. College graduation turned out to be one the most joyful occasions of my life, though it could not have been further from the day I had envisioned for years. I would not have wanted it any other way.

I learned a great deal about stoicism, resiliency, and strength by the example Dad provided during his illness. Equally important was how I saw Mom, a strong woman I admire and look up to, facing down every imaginable threat to her family. Just witnessing the way she made sure I had the best possible ending to college life while managing the household and caring for Dad—this was a huge lesson about strong families, strong women, motherhood, and the pure power of love.

FRANK'S JOURNAL

I WANT MY HEALTH. It's really that simple: I want my health, energy, and very essence back. As it says in Mark 9:23, "everything is possible for him that believes." I must believe with all my heart and soul that I will return to full health, and I know everything is possible. My apprehension, my fear, is that I will somehow regress and have the rug pulled out from under me.

Just look at how far I've come in a little over a month. I'm feeling healthier and stronger each day. Each day has been better than the one before, at least for the past week. No stigma, no disease, just the ease of knowing that my life will get better and back to—not back to a new normal but forward to a more frequent extraordinary. It's going to be OK, and I will return to being the happy person I've always been. I rejoice in knowing that I am loved, and I will fully heal my mind and body.

DO IT: DISIDENTIFY

- Don't renounce your adversity. Stop fighting it. See through it. Become aware of the reason you have allowed it into your life and seen it as some indominable force, and it will eventually drop from your hands. You don't chase darkness out of the room with a knife or a broom; instead, you turn on the light. Through understanding, adversity slowly disappears.

- Recognize all adversity, from a minor financial or relational setback to being diagnosed with a serious disease, as the temporary condition that it is. You are the blue sky. All adversities are the dark clouds that *will* pass by.

- Progress is incremental and comes with baby steps and backsliding. Backsliding into denialism is to be expected. These are the early days of facing down your adversity. You will prevail!

You don't chase darkness out of the room with a knife or a broom; instead, you turn on the light.

VIOLATE FATE

Look for Possibilities at
The Fringe of Impossible

*In which our hero takes having a bad hair day
to a whole new level.*

Early in his career as a real estate artist, Frank was featured on the cover of *USA Today* with his most expensive oceanfront spec home to date. The article quoted an MIT economics professor: "That young man will soon be dumpster diving. There is no market for a spec home with those features offered at that price."

To be sure, that expert had all kinds of advanced degrees and a background in finance and real estate, while Frank never even went to college and graduated from his fourth high school with a 1.8 GPA. But Frank proved the professor wrong, and then he went so far as to send the man a photo of himself standing in a dumpster after he closed the $30 million sale.

Just 28 days after the *USA Today* article came out, Frank mailed him the photo with a note: *I guess you were right, professor. I am dumpster diving, but I'm doing so with a big fat check in my hand!*

He's never been afraid to violate accepted wisdom, or disagree, loudly, with conventional authorities when facing adversity.

* * *

You must challenge, even change, the mind of fate itself. Whose fate? The one that others, who may be well-intentioned, project upon you. In creating your own reality, one of the biggest challenges is that your future is constantly being created or influenced by outside forces too numerous to count. Some good: loving parents or a spouse who want only the best for you. Some bad: a business partner or lover who spews negativity and leaves you high and dry.

We must all become aware of the instances when someone is projecting their own ideas of our personal fate into the deepest synapses of our subconscious. Pay attention, or you'll never recognize how insidious this can become. But when you see it, reject others' negative ideas about who you are or who they think you were born to be.

"You're the smart one, and your sister is the pretty one."

"Your brother's the businessman, and you're the artist."

"You'll never amount to anything. You're such a screw-up. Just a loser."

> **We must all become aware of the instances
> when someone is projecting their own ideas
> of our personal fate into the deepest synapses
> of our subconscious.**

These are some of the fates projected upon so many kids, and it can take a lifetime to deconstruct these messages that have been tattooed into a subconscious narrative.

* * *

Frank has written and spoken about killing the person he was supposedly born to be: a banker like his father and grandfather before him. Or a career criminal, because in his youth he had the unfortunate habit of getting arrested repeatedly and thrown into juvenile detention. One reason Frank eventually straightened out and went on a meteoric tear to become a successful real estate artist, bestselling author, ultramarathoner, philanthro-capitalist, and family man is that his own father had never projected any fate upon him. Frank had projected the notion of becoming a banker on himself, because of course Frank McKinney III would be a banker! Third generation, what else would he become? After some serious acting out that landed him in juvie seven times, it appeared that perhaps a life of crime would be his path.

In fact, though, the fate of neither the banker nor the criminal was even remotely close to the life he created for himself.

And now, Frank's condition threatens to end it all. He is nowhere near out of the woods, and the usual fate for those facing this particular intruder is quite discouraging. So with his customary flourish, Frank whips out his own prescription pad, selects a pen with ink that's visible only to the fate *he* chooses, and writes his own destiny. Again.

He will not fight or override sound medical advice, but from the start he has decided that this journey will be a collaboration. Frank's doctors know all about the risks, probable outcomes, and likely side effects of his aggressive treatment. They have a good feel for general statistical results and timetables. In addition to their extensive medical training, they also have access to the latest information about new treatments and drug trials. The doctors have seen tens of thousands of patients with this diagnosis. But there is only one Frank McKinney, just like there is only one of each of us. Frank has an intimate relationship with all 37.2 trillion cells in his body and a keen understanding of every aspect of his being.

> **Frank whips out his own prescription pad, selects a pen with ink that's visible only to the fate *he* chooses, and writes his own destiny.**

Never one for the averages, medians, or means in life, as always he seeks the outliers, those positive possibilities at the fringe of impossible. So no, he won't focus on the man who was diagnosed on a Friday and died within a week. He's going to look to the woman who was treated, followed a plan, and was miraculously and completely restored to health in a month. Neither outcome is particularly likely for Frank, but he knows which one he's going for.

Never one for the averages, medians, or means in life, as always he seeks the outliers, those positive possibilities at the fringe of impossible.

With his faith in God and through the collaboration with his doctor, he will determine his own fate, make his own miracle.

* * *

The ancient Greeks believed that the Fates controlled every human destiny: Three goddesses determined whatever happiness, tragedy, joy, or sorrow someone experienced, including whether that person was a king or a slave. They portioned out and spun the threads of human life, and when Atropos snipped a thread with her scissors, that life ended. People simply accepted what happened to them as the whim and will of the Fates, believing it was completely out of their hands.

This is the opposite of contemporary American thinking. Today we would wonder, *Why in the world would you ever allow someone else to take the wheel when it's your life?* Even so, in moments of adversity, your subconscious will scream at you to accept a fate projected upon you by your doctor, spouse, child, business partner, lover, lawyer. Don't do it. Do your best to make the most informed decisions, to create a pattern and upward cycle of empowerment, not victimhood.

* * *

Frank is not about to let go of the controls. He will hold on for dear life and fly that rocket ship through this freaking meteor storm with Nilsa and Dr. Eduardo Garcia at his side.

Only a few months into this journey, Frank is still very much afraid, sometimes terrified. Violating fate is a months-long process of negotiation and collaboration, trial and error, two steps forward and two steps back. It is a gift from God that Dr. Garcia is the one, out of all the doctors in the world, who arrives to collaborate on Frank's fate. No journey is ever taken alone, and this man is truly heaven-sent.

N ILSA'S STORY

Our weekly trips to check the bloodwork and numbers were Frank's only ventures out for several months, and they were initially rough going. At the beginning, of course, Frank could barely move. One day we had an appointment at 9 a.m., and he was in such bad shape that, after numerous attempts and false starts, I could not rally him up and out of bed until 3 that afternoon. It's not that he didn't want to go; he was eager for the weekly update. But he could not force his body to do something for which it was simply not ready. We managed to arrive just in time for the very last appointment at the end of that afternoon.

The days all started to blend together, and trips to the doctor's office were especially challenging. We were still under lockdown, and I was trying like hell to keep him out of the hospital. It made me nervous to even bring him in for his checkups. Attempting to support and carry my feverish, sickly husband down the steps from our room to the car, then get him settled and buckled in, was a production.

He usually slumped forward against the seat belt in the car as I drove. I always carried a bag full of stuff Frank might need: bottled water, Gatorade, apple slices, ice packs. Whatever it was, I had it handy. It reminded me of when Laura was a newborn, and I had my ever-present diaper bag. With Frank, who was about 10 times the size our little one had been, I would be wiped out by the time we made it to the parking lot, and we weren't even inside the doctor's office yet!

Prior to and even after we started seeing Dr. Garcia, Frank had been through the expected stages: denial, disbelief, anger. But during every stage he had made it clear he would handle this his way, not the way everyone else did it, even if it came to the point of him considering not taking medication or possibly seeking out nontraditional healing. Fortunately, Dr. Garcia was on board with Frank's refusal to identify with the disease. After the first day he never referred to the official diagnosis again in our presence. He understood and approved Frank's desire to disidentify.

In addition to being gifted in his medical craft, Dr. Garcia was gentle, caring, loving, and genuinely invested in and committed to all his patients. His bedside manner was unparalleled: patient in moments of frustration and physical duress, always with the time to listen empathetically, always making it clear we were on this journey together. Truly a guardian angel. I had Dr. Garcia's cell phone number, and there were times I needed to call him about managing Frank's fluctuating symptoms and side effects. Frank always held my hand and counted on me to help get him past the latest crisis. Dr. Garcia gave me the confidence to do what I had to do, as I knew help was only a text away. He was always available and responded quickly. He cared about Frank and me. He was such a gift.

If I were to sculpt a doctor who would be able to able to manage Frank's drive, personality, and general inability to conform, this man would be it. He was tailor-made for the role. Given what we were up against, it is not going too far to say that Frank may not have made it without Dr. Garcia. A collaboration with a different doctor would likely have led, sooner or later, to Frank rebelling and bolting. It never came to that.

When I had moments alone with Dr. Garcia, he spoke freely about the disease to me, using its official name, but that was just the two of us in private discussions. He never called it by name in front of Frank. He was always sensitive and aware, which is all you can hope for in a doctor. As compassionate and empathetic as he was, he was also firm. There were lines he would not cross, no matter what Frank said or wanted. He was explicit on those issues he felt strongly about, yet he always listened to Frank's suggestions. Nine times out of 10 he found a compromise between what he felt was medically necessary and what Frank needed to keep hope alive on his recovery journey.

Early on, Dr. Garcia said to me, "It's important that Frank never feels he is losing control of his health." I could not have agreed more. It was going to be a long road to recovery. We were on the same page. We could not have asked for a better doctor.

Laura has graduated, Dr. Garcia is a godsend, and the medicine is doing its job. All told, things are on the upswing. Frank is even starting to put on some weight. He's done with Gleevec, the "chemo in a bottle" they sent home with him when he left the hospital. Now he's on Sprycel, another chemotherapy pill, and little by little, with constant negotiation, they are gradually decreasing the dosage.

**Hair and body are thinning, looking more like a
PEZ dispenser than a rock star**

On the extensive list of possible side effects for Sprycel, hair loss is way down at the bottom and unlikely to occur. Yet Frank's hair starts coming out by the handful, enough to stop up the shower drain. The first time this happens, he lets out a howl of anguish and bursts into tears, the kind he has not cried since he was a child: face red, unable to catch his breath, tears streaming down his face, sobbing uncontrollably, inconsolable. Nilsa hears his cry from the second-floor shower all the way down in the kitchen and bolts upstairs, sure he must be lying on the floor dying. He's taken a clump of hair out of the shower and dropped it next to the sink. It's a wad as big as a baseball!

**He lets out a howl of anguish and bursts into tears,
the kind he has not cried since he was a child:
face red, unable to catch his breath, tears
streaming down his face, sobbing
uncontrollably, inconsolable.**

This can't be happening! I can't be losing my hair! But more comes out every time he steps into the shower or tries to run a comb through what used to be thick, long locks. His hair has been a sure thing since he was a kid: he's always had great hair, and a lot of it. And because his hair is such a large part of Frank's brand, this loss hits him harder than anything else. Of course, many patients who get chemotherapy are left with thin, wispy strands. Some shave it off in an act of strength and defiance: *Screw it! I'm bald.* Some see the hair loss as the least of their concerns. But it slays Frank. *Now this?!* One more indignity.

FRANK'S JOURNAL

Will I have my condition for the rest of my life, the next two years, or both? I hope it's neither. I know it's not easy, but I must believe that I won't be on this medication, or have this condition, for life. Lord, I am so grateful for how far I have come. It was only a little over three months ago I was admitted to the hospital, and look where I am now. Why does it seem like it's not enough, like I haven't come far enough?

I know why. The primary reason is my hair.

It causes me trauma as I watch it fall out every single day. Why this too? Why does it mean that much to me? I have always seen my hair as part of my brand, and not having it makes it hard on me. I had a lot of fun changing the colors, style . . . Yes, my hair, all aspects of it, brought me tons of joy and confidence. To see it vanish at this rate is devastating. I pray, Lord, that you return my hair to the full healthy state I once enjoyed. You say, Lord, that you "make our hearts for joy" and that we "won't lose treasures that truly matter." Well, my hair really matters to me; it has been my treasure all my life. So, I guess I can deal with a lack of energy, but I can't deal with no hair!

I realize how much my hair means to me, and that's perfectly OK. It's OK that I get emotional about it, that I want it back yesterday. Why? Because it brought me joy. I had great times going into Dawn's color room and mixing up new shades. It was so much fun to change every couple of months. It made me feel different, unique, happy. The amount of hair loss over the last few months is crushing. One more pressure. One more straw on this aging camel's back.

I have a plan and must accept the reality that I will wear a hairpiece or wig for the next few years while I strive for complete molecular remission and, eventually, treatment-free remission.

I will have good days and bad, and I need to realize that this is inevitable. I will lean into God and ask for help, even with my hair. Yes, Lord, please stop this hair loss! I am believing in a healthy head of hair you will again place on my head. For you have counted each hair on my head, and you know the number I have lost. You know the number to return to my head! You know the joy my hair brings to my life, and you never let us lose the treasures that really matter.

Even though the doctor, Nilsa, and Laura see a difference in him, Frank doesn't feel enough of an improvement. He can barely run. He has very little energy. The sparkle that was his life has not returned, and the hair loss is the biggest blow, the one that pushes him over the edge. He wonders, *Is this going to be the rest of my life, shuffling around in a perpetual state of lethargy while losing all my hair?* Frank absolutely will not live like that. He spends many dark mornings and nights weeping in the shower as more hair falls to the tiled floor and washes toward the clogged drain.

And then he and Nilsa take action. It is not his fate to be a bald man!

Nilsa does a bit of research then goes to a large wig shop in Boca Raton to snap photos of the best possible options. Frank reviews them on his phone, and she brings two of them home. The next day Frank talks his stylist, Dawn Edwards, into meeting Nilsa and him at her shop, which is still closed tight due to COVID restrictions. They meet in the dark of night for a secret appointment. As these are women's wigs, Dawn needs to cut and color them both to suit Frank's unusual style. He tries them on to see how they look. A wig looks a little odd, a little funny, but it's a huge relief. It feels so good to have a lot of hair again!

The wig before . . .   **And the wig after the secret rendezvous at the salon**

It goes OK for a while, wearing the wigs. They are necessary because the world is starting to open back up after the launch of a COVID vaccine. As time passes, Frank ventures out to meet people and posts on social media. In person and in photos, the hair looks fine. After all, the public is used to seeing Frank sporting different hairstyles in unusual colors. He can certainly tell the difference but hopes nobody else can. However, wearing a wig is a pain. In a heavy wind it could shift or blow right off his head! This is worrisome, as Frank is starting to show prospective buyers a $15 million oceanfront project he has for sale, and the last thing he needs is his wig flying into the pool.

This ongoing hair saga is taking "bad hair days" to a whole new level. Plain and simple, Frank is wigging out.

Even though he is on the mend, he simply cannot continue this wig routine any longer, so Nilsa reaches out to Dr. Alan Bauman, a world-renowned hair doctor who had kept Frank's natural hair so healthy and abundant with a complicated regimen of platelet-rich plasma therapy, vitamins, hormones, and scalp treatments. A head of hair like Frank's at his age didn't just happen or come cheaply. Now he needs another solution, and Dr. Bauman finds one for him. It's another successful collaboration with fate.

Dr. Bauman suggests the absolute highest-end type of hair prosthesis, the kind movie stars wear. These hair pieces are created in Europe, taking months to make and using human hair to the precise measurements of the client's scalp. The prosthesis is then permanently glued to the head, and the wearer can shower, style it, color it, swim, run, stand in the wind, and it's not going anywhere. This is the Rolls-Royce of hair replacement.

And since Frank is willing to give his left testicle to get his hair back—heck, he'd sell a kidney, you name it—this is a no-brainer. Frank even gets to pick the thickness, curl, and length of this beautiful don't-call-it-a-wig.

They take the head measurements, and Frank pays a premium to have two pieces rushed to his Florida home from overseas. Dr. Bauman applies one, and this new system works great for a while, but then Frank starts to feel claustrophobic and worries about what's happening to whatever's left of his real hair, smothered under all this glue and a prosthetic hairpiece. Frank thinks, *I'm going to get better someday and want my own hair back.*

So, after about eight weeks, this not-a-wig experiment is over, and Dr. Bauman frees Frank from the beautiful but oppressive thing. Frank donates the two prostheses he'd bought to a cancer charity, where he hopes they will brighten another patient's day.

And so he is back to a wig when he wants "show hair" but can take it off whenever he needs a break—or as soon as his own hair regrows. High winds be damned.

*   *   *

For years, Frank and Nilsa have been friendly with 80-year-old Vincent, a man who used to be homeless. Born in Philadelphia, Vinny was raised in 27 different foster homes that ranged from bad to horrendous, although he can still recall the name of the *one* foster mom, Katherine, who was kind to him. It has been a tough life for Vinny, but Frank, Nilsa, and Laura have done their best to help him over the years by finding then paying for his small efficiency apartment in Lake Worth, Florida. In the

Nilsa, Frank, and Vinny

interest of returning to some socializing and a regular schedule, Frank and Nilsa meet him for a picnic one afternoon.

FRANK'S JOURNAL

Will someone hand me a yellow balloon? Just one small random expression of good fortune that comes my way and puts a smile on my face?

We had a wonderful time at a picnic to celebrate Vinny's birthday today. It was simple and joyous, with blessings exchanged between friends. We shared our faith and happiness in being together. At the end of the party, while we were pushing Vinny back to his apartment in his wheelchair, I saw three girls riding their skateboards. We had three balloons left over from the party, so I gave each girl one. To the youngest girl, maybe 6 years old, I gave a yellow balloon. The look of pure excitement and happiness on the little girl's face for something so simple left me longing to experience the same.

My fear and stress are so high; I've been told I should take these dreaded pills for the rest of my life. I just want one day where I smile because I didn't expect a random act of kindness or good fortune. At times I seem so close to having my life back, yet at others it seems so, so hard. Will someone please hand me just one yellow balloon? That would be nice.

The collaboration with Dr. Garcia is going well, and it is always lively. Frank doesn't just sit there, nodding. He goes in loaded with the latest information and asks question after question, always thinking outside the box, just as he had done when he was first consulting specialists about the stem cell procedure on his knee.

Back then he asked, "Can we get stem cells from an Olympic athlete versus some random donor?"

The doctor—not the one who later did the procedure—looked at Frank like he was nuts. "No, you will get the stem cells that come in from our lab."

Why did the man think this was such a crazy request? If they were going to inject foreign stem cells in Frank's body, why should they not be the absolute best he can find for the intended purpose? Someone who wouldn't consider thinking outside the box, nor explain why a box was even necessary, was not the doctor for Frank, clearly. At that point in his life, Frank was no longer collaborating with anyone with whom he did not personally connect. He did not care what kind of talented builder, brilliant architect, creative moviemaker, or medical specialist they might be. Then as now, there had to be a collaborative magnetism and energy from the start.

So he had moved on from this doctor's closed-minded approach and found his trusted orthopedist, Dr. Jorge Gonzalez, who chose to use Frank's own stem cells.

"Forget what the MRI says about the cartilage in your knee," he once told Frank. "We're not even going to look at the scans. What I want to know is how do you feel? How's the knee holding up these days, and how can I help you to keep doing what you love?"

Now that is practicing medicine, not just putting up an X-ray that shows zero cartilage in the knee joint and prescribing medicine or surgery so Frank could walk to the end of his driveway to get his mail. No, Frank's knees were supposed to carry him 135 miles in the Death Valley desert.

Still, in these dark days, Frank wonders about his novel procedure. Had his aggressive experimenting opened the door and let the intruder in? Had it awakened a dormant beast? This mystery may never be solved in Frank's lifetime, though he plans to ask God should he get the opportunity. Even if he is no longer on this earth, Frank will be curious to know how all this came about. He's dying to know. He will have to die to know.

Given this life-or-death situation, he trusts his fruitful give-and-take with his oncologist, Dr. Garcia, who happily entertains the collaborative dance that happens every time they meet. This doctor is always ready to engage him. He always asks questions that truly resonate with Frank: *How are your energy levels? Your vitality? How are your running times? Your hair loss: how much is in the brush at night? How is your appetite?* Those are the real markers, the questions that matter, more important than anything bloodwork might show.

As Frank's numbers are really starting to improve, he is constantly negotiating to cut his Sprycel dosages. He is on a strong dosage of 100 mg, and it's working on one level, but the red blood cell and platelet counts (the good ones that give him his energy) are being obliterated.

So Frank says, "Let's cut it."

Dr. Garcia says, "You're not ready."

Frank tries again. "Let's keep it at 100 but do it every other day."

The doctor agrees, and Frank's red blood cell count goes in the wrong direction. Frank is dejected.

Dr. Garcia says, "Frank, I agree with you about not going back to 100. But I think your body needs a significant dosage of this medicine every day, not skipping any. Instead of 100 every other day, we're going to try 50 every day."

The first day of the failed every-other-day trial had been the first time in months Frank hadn't taken a pill. It is a blow to go back to medicating every single day and a daily reminder of what he is living with, but the results are incredible! The next time he goes in for bloodwork a month later, the numbers associated with his diagnosis are getting better!

Frank continues to seek collaboration, though sometimes, the doctor responds with, "Frank, it's just not time."

"But my energy levels. But my running is starting to come back. But my hair. But, but, but . . ."

"Frank, it's not time."

Back and forth, back and forth. If Dr. Garcia is adamant, Frank acquiesces with tears of frustration.

Dr. Garcia is always quick to console. "Frank, I hate to see you upset like this. I understand how you feel, but you are not ready."

Frank accepts this. *Must* accept this. He never walks out of Dr. Garcia's office saying, "Eff this, I'm going to cut my pills in half and do it my way." He is never that reckless or rebellious, never ready to say, "I'm just going to do my own thing," as they always manage to arrive at a consensus.

Frank is not used to practicing patience when he doesn't want to. His family and doctors might be delighted with his progress, but Frank is deeply mourning the loss of his hair, and his energy levels still aren't where he wants them. He wants it all back now. At this point, he goes out to get a second opinion. The funny thing is that Dr. Garcia probably knows about it almost immediately, as there is only a small circle of local doctors in this specialty.

The new doctor looks at all the bloodwork and reviews all the numbers as Frank says, "There's gotta be an alternative to this. I am tired. Tired of feeling tired, and tired of my hair falling out! Is Dr. Garcia doing the right thing and, assuming he is, isn't there a lesser dose?"

The doctor assures him that if she were diagnosed with Frank's condition, Dr. Garcia is the only specialist she would seek out. This new doctor tells him there is a 20 mg dose of Sprycel, which she prescribes for a patient who normally weighs under 100 pounds and could not tolerate anything stronger. Frank brings this information right back to Dr. Garcia, along with photo proof of the medicine's existence, and they move ahead.

Good doctors want to be challenged. They want to learn from their patients. Unfortunately, many doctors have become accustomed to being comfortable playing God and calling the shots on someone's fate because so few patients have the courage to create then pursue their own.

NILSA'S STORY

The best example of what I witnessed between Frank and Dr. Garcia was a visit when Frank was not feeling great even though his numbers were improving ever so slowly. Dr. Garcia entered the room, greeted us pleasantly as always, opened his computer and said, "Frank, I have some fantastic news. Your numbers are really improving," and laid them out. Frank was so overwhelmed by the considerable progress and good news that he broke down on the examination table and started to cry.

I immediately stood up to go console Frank, but Dr. Garcia beat me to it. To see our doctor genuinely so happy for Frank, saying, "See, see, we are going to get there!"—it was the sweetest exchange. Such a happy moment, a moment where I was so grateful that God had whispered this man into our world. Dr. Garcia allowed us to believe and hope that everything was going to be OK again.

Every week, then every month, both of us held our breath, waiting to see how the bloodwork would turn out. All we wanted was to see those crucial numbers improve. Oh, those texts! "Great news, Frank! Numbers getting soooooo much better!" Because Dr. Garcia knew what good news did for Frank's spirits, he would even send a screen capture of the numbers before they hit Frank's portal. Then, after many months, we started seeing readings that were really improving, meaning lots of high-fiving and true joy in our house. We still had a ways to go, but Dr. Garcia enjoyed these victories as much as we did. We cherished his texts. He always gave Frank enough of what he wanted, what he needed. Frank never lost hope or control of his own fate. It was no longer doctor-patient. They—we—were a team.

FRANK'S JOURNAL

I now see what I have as a special condition, not just a condition. Yes, the uninvited guest has become a special one to me. Now that my bloodwork really is improving, I will refer to this as a special condition. Still, I want to forget altogether that I have this special blessing. I do need to keep seeing this condition as a blessing for what it has given me. It's a blessing because now I cherish something that I took for granted all my life: my health.

TIME FOR YOU TO VIOLATE FATE

- Challenge then change the mind of fate itself. You and only you will make the final determination of your fate, especially when faced with physical, financial, or relational adversity. Remember: Your fate comes from within, not without.

- Actively seek out someone whose magnetism and energy allows for the best possible collaboration on the fate of your current adversity. If you must, go it alone until you find this person or persons, but find them soon.

- The fewer collaborators on your fate the better when facing adversity. You're already halfway out of your mind: dying, getting divorced, losing a loved one, losing your home, losing your business, stubbing your toe, whatever the case may be. One or two trusted collaborators are all you need, because ultimately YOU are the one in charge.

EVERY. SINGLE. DAY.

Methodically Apply the Mundane

When you first picked up this book and turned to page one, you could not have imagined the progress you've now made!

Talk about the ultimate blank slate: Gutzon Borglum, the sculptor who carved four U.S. presidents' faces onto Mount Rushmore in the remote Black Hills of South Dakota, encountered extreme adversity with his new commission. But Borglum, renowned for his "distinctly American" art style, accepted and rose to the challenge. He disidentified from impediments and naysayers too numerous to count. He most certainly violated fate by disregarding the accepted wisdom that said such a work could never be accomplished, especially not by a 57-year-old man. Oh, and that man would be using simple hammers and chisels, as there were no modern power tools back in 1920s when he began his herculean task. Borglum consulted others on which presidents to include, surveyed the area numerous times, made many preliminary drawings and sketches, then packed his simple tools into a worn-out old leather case and showed up on day one, October 4, 1927, at the vast granite outcroppings. And he would show up every single day thereafter for 14 years until his work was complete in 1941.

Ideally this is where you have now progressed with your current adversity, whether it's physical, financial, spiritual, or relational—whatever condition has left you just barely hanging on, at the end of your rope. You have used denialism then accepted your struggle. You have also disidentified with the circumstance, meaning you're refusing to give it any of your power and precious energy, and you and your collaborator(s) are choosing to violate fate. Now what?

Imagine the enormity of the task set before Borglum on his very first day. And what did he do? Well, he rolled up his sleeves and started chipping away, one chisel stroke at a time. In other words, he got to work, and he kept working for the next 14 years. (When he died as the sculptures were nearing completion, his son took over and finished.)

Two months into the project, an observer from below would not have been able to see even one eyebrow hair on what would become George Washington's enormous face. Borglum's progress was imperceptible, done bit by bit, chiseling away day by day, every single day. Over 5,000 days later, Mount Rushmore was complete, one of the most enduring monuments in the United States and an instantly recognizable symbol of America across the world. It will stand for centuries.

You will turn this adversity around, but only through proactive application of the nine steps in this book.

Whatever adversity you are suffering or will suffer, it is highly unlikely that it will become your personal Mount Rushmore, but remember, it's up to you to carve the results you desire. You are staring at a bleak mountain face and carrying a small pack of tools that seem pitifully not up to the job. It's time to pull them out and get on with it.

You will turn this adversity around, but only through proactive application of the nine steps in this book. Even if you go down in flames—your spouse leaves and takes the kids, the dog, and your goldfish—you lose your business or home in bankruptcy or in a lawsuit you've been fighting for years—you don't get the promotion you deserve or the retirement you've planned or the chance to compete at the level you aspire to—whatever it is—at least you'll go down fighting and with a sense of purpose. If you get divorced or break up, you can find someone else to love, even remarry. If you lose all your money, you can eventually earn more than the thousands or millions of dollars you lost. If you can't seem to get ahead in one endeavor, you can shift your focus to something new and perhaps something more joyful. Outside of some sudden and unforeseen occurrence of death, only a serious health condition could prove truly fatal, and if so, you'd enjoy heaven and be out of pain. Remember the blue sky? All is fleeting in the big picture of a life. One of the most critical yet simple keys to success lies in getting out there and plugging away every single day.

* * *

Frank is now back to his regular workouts, including walking on the treadmill inside his 170-degree sauna. His rapid progress is unquestionably due to the fact that he follows his routine, without fail, every single day. Whether he manages to drag himself across the street for one block or a mile, it all adds up to this: one red-letter day when Frank makes it back to running six miles (a 10K) in an hour and 40 minutes. This is truly cause for celebration. He's really picking up the pace! This 100 minutes is twice the amount of time it would take him in optimum health, but relentless forward motion is working. And it takes off from there.

Before acquiring his special condition, Frank's off-season exercise routine would mean running six miles and going to the gym on alternating days and taking Sundays off. (In training for a race, the regimen would get much tougher.) Now, as he works up to this goal, Frank usually comes back from his run and collapses onto a lounge chair on his wooden deck by the pool. On the wall inside the kitchen door hangs an 18-inch crucifix, a gift from a monk at his 11th grade boarding school, that means the world to him. Often Frank carefully unhooks the crucifix, brings it out to his lounge chair, and holds onto it for dear life, sometimes managing to take a nap in these early morning hours just as the sun is starting to come up. He is not sleeping well at night, but curled up with the crucifix held close to his chest he is sometimes able to rest peacefully for about an hour.

Frank also prays the Holy Rosary every single day using the prayer beads gifted to him by St. Pope John Paul II.

Nearly 20 years earlier, he, Nilsa, and Laura were granted a private audience with His Eminence in Rome. As they sat in the inner sanctum of the Vatican awaiting their turn, Frank was restless as usual, nervously prowling around the lavish study. Then he headed toward a beautiful and massive window that opened onto a small balcony.

When Frank cranked open the window, he gazed outward over Vatican City and all of Rome. He had no idea that he was standing in the spot made famous in hundreds of newscasts as the place where the pope unfurls the papal regalia and stands to address the huge crowds who come to see him speak. So when the Italians and tourists down in the square looked up, they saw Frank standing there, his long, curly, dirty-blond hair down to his shoulders.

They started shouting, "Look, it's Jesus!"

In the blink of an eye a large crowd gathered and some people pointed upward with one hand and covered their mouths in disbelief with the other.

Frank waved and smiled until Nilsa rushed over and whispered to him, "Francisco, get back in here and close that window. Show some respect!"

Fortunately, the pope never saw any of this. During their 30-minute private meeting, the pope gave Frank, Nilsa, and Laura each a rosary that he personally blessed. One of Nilsa's closest friends had a child with leukemia who was on death's doorstep, so she asked the pope to please say a personal prayer for this desperately ill child, as well as his heartbroken parents.

For years and years after that trip, and certainly every single day of his illness, Frank would take the prayer beads from his bedside on many mornings and recite the Holy Rosary. Over time, the beads have become chipped, and the crucifix hangs by a thread due to daily wear and tear.

In the Catholic faith, this rosary from St. Pope John Paul II is what is known as a second-class relic: something touched or used by a saint in his lifetime. Frank is a man of faith. He often wears the pope's rosary around his neck and has hung it from the rearview mirror of the crew vehicle in all

St. Pope John Paul II in his study giving Frank the special rosary

12 of his Badwater races. He is a firm believer in the power of prayer and believes we should all ask God for what we want—then get up and go after it! Romans 5:3–5 says, " . . . but we also glory in our sufferings, because we know that suffering produces perseverance; perseverance, character; and character, hope." He believes we must persevere, never lose hope, because hope never disappoints.

In the darkest of times, Nilsa's friend whose child had leukemia never lost hope, and their son is now a happy, healthy 20-something. A modern-day miracle attributable to the pope's prayer? That's another question Frank plans to ask when he gets to heaven.

In his book *The Tap*, Frank exhorted his readers in chapter 5 to "get off your knees and start walking." Straight from the gospel of Frank McKinney: God won't do for you what you can already do for yourself. He has given you many gifts, including the ability to do amazing things that only seem impossible. Many poor, suffering souls are inside church or at their bedside on their knees when already they have everything they need to go out and pursue exactly what they are praying for!

* * *

The good news: Several months of applying relentless forward motion every single day is not hard to do, and the rewards can be incredible. Inching forward, day by day, committing to making small efforts every single day can and will mitigate your current adversity! The bad news: This is often the point where so many people abandon the A-D-V-E-R-S-I-T-Y plan, when they just can't seem to stick to whatever new routine they have put in place, whether it's financial, relational, spiritual, physical, dietary, vice-related (giving up something like alcohol or sugar), an exercise or meditation routine, or something else.

Commitment to doing something every single day gets derailed for only one of two reasons: attention deficit (AD) or boredom.

1. ATTENTION DEFICIT

Our entire society now suffers from AD, often with hyperactivity thrown in. The National Institute of Mental Health estimates that only 3 to 5 percent of the population meets the official criteria for a diagnosis of Attention Deficit Hyperactivity Disorder (ADHD), but you wouldn't know it from just looking around at most everyone you know. Those who suffer from clinical ADHD struggle with restlessness, feeling overwhelmed, being easily distractible, and loss of impulse control. They find it hard to finish tasks and follow through on commitments, experiencing everything as just "too much" and overwhelming. Doesn't this sound like a lot of people at least some of the time? Does this sound like you on occasion? Most *all* of us have some form of nonclinical AD, or simple attention deficit issues.

AD is kryptonite to commitment.
This "every single day" thing is not too much,
yet it means everything.

AD is a significant impediment to our pursuit of joy these days because it's so easy to get distracted by those four screens mentioned earlier: the phone, the computer, the tablet, and the television. We are distracted by social media, checking the likes on our posts, watching YouTube and TikTok videos. It's a soothing and easy escape just a click away—and it's a distraction. To overcome adversity when you're hanging on by a thread, success requires that you minimize distractions and roll up your sleeves. AD is kryptonite to commitment. This "every single day" thing is not too much, yet it means everything.

2. BOREDOM

There is another reason applying the *every single day* approach can fail. It's because the day-in, day-out everydayness of any new routine quickly becomes tedious, unexciting, dull. Easily distractible humans are soon bored and distracted by the latest new shiny object. Sticking to a routine takes commitment, day after "boring" day.

By now you've done the hard work. Look at how far you've come with your current adversity. Do *not* allow AD or boredom (or a likely combination of both) to take over. Focus on what you must do. When AD or boredom begins to creep in, ask yourself one simple question: *Do I want to go backward or stick to the A-D-V-E-R-S-I-T-Y program and continue to move forward?* Yes, sometimes sticking to the program is hard. Life is effing hard! It's not fun to backslide and have to start over. (Ask anyone who has lost 20 pounds and regained 30 or who has relapsed into addiction.) Don't allow yourself to get bored or distracted and let the whole house of cards tumble again. The results you are seeing now were aspirational to you only a short time ago. Now, they *are* real. Don't lose them!

*L*AURA'S STORY

My father is a creature of habit. For as long as I can remember he showed me the power of simply setting a routine and sticking to it. Going to bed and rising at the same time nearly every day. Walking me to school every day until I went to high school. All the simple day-to-day tasks he completed religiously were a comforting ritual and a big part of my childhood. They were simply second nature to him.

Every single night growing up I would be in my room getting ready to go to sleep when I'd hear the sound of a metal spoon clanging against the inside of an old-fashioned large metal cup, the oversized kind they used to mix drugstore malts in. Dad has had this battered cup since he was a kid in boarding school, and he uses it to mix his magic power potions before he goes to bed.

"Good night, Ppeekk," he would call after the refrigerator door shut. Every morning like clockwork I would be awakened by the sound of the blender as he mixed up his special morning concoction, same time every day. (Early!)

Something else that got my attention as a kid was the gradual realization that every week Dad would create a priority sheet. He would write a list of the most pressing matters coming up that he needed to stay on top of. He might complete them that week, or some would be pushed forward to the next, but each item was written down, reread each night, and checked off when completed. I was fascinated by this businesslike approach. To the public, Dad was always a larger-than-life, over-the-top kind of figure, and it all appeared so completely spontaneous. I saw behind the scenes: the discipline, work, and practice it took to appear so passionate and unrehearsed when it was showtime.

When I was about six years old, Dad began his sauna workouts in preparation for his first Badwater ultramarathon. In front of his treadmill, in chalk on the wall, Dad wrote the words *relentless forward motion* at eye level. This message was right there in his face as he completed his brutal treadmill workouts in our 170-degree sauna. I was mightily impressed by this powerful phrase, and the words penetrated my subconscious. *Relentless forward motion* certainly sums up every single day of my dad's life! It's how he managed to get through business setbacks, being unable to finish a Badwater race, and life's personal problems. Those are the three words Dad lives by, and they serve him well.

I saw behind the scenes: the discipline, work, and practice it took to appear so passionate and unrehearsed when it was showtime.

The sauna mantra

When I get stuck in a rut, or frustrated, those three words come to me. I know that when the going gets tough, with relentless forward motion I will eventually get past any obstacles. Dad's health condition did not change his approach, either. He simply adjusted it and ramped it up. And I must laugh, because these days, as an adult, I start every single day with my own special drink in my own juicer. Early. Same mix every day, like clockwork.

Relentless forward motion certainly sums up every single day of my dad's life!

FRANK'S JOURNAL

I have a fantastic way to begin my new journal! A while ago, I wrote that I wanted to attain major molecular remission, not really knowing what that meant. Well, now I do. I learned today that my PCR test, after only five months of my condition, came back at 0.134 percent, this after starting out at 46.6 percent! The goal was to be under 1 percent, and I'm under that by 86.6 percent. And, with the ecstatic news of being at 0.134 percent, I am just barely over the 0.100 percent needed to attain major molecular remission!

Now I'm remembering months ago when I couldn't even get out of my bed to go to the bathroom. I could have died. This latest news has lifted my spirits tremendously. From praying my Rosary, getting out on the road every day, getting in the sauna, eating well: God will not let us lose treasures that truly matter. I treasure my health and at this rate I will have it back! All I can say is thank you, Lord. My health returning is the greatest treasure you could ever give me.

It is one of those brief moments that shows that the glory and mercy of God endures, even in life's toughest times. Today, sitting in the chair across from my bed and looking at the spot where I was sick and dying only a few short months ago now brings me immense joy. It's OK to believe fully now. Let all that hesitation go. The Lord has delivered me from death.

It's OK to believe fully now.

Let all that hesitation go.

He has done so in more than just the physical sense. He has saved my soul and my body. My body will eventually die, but now my soul will live on in heaven forever. But just not yet! I have a book to write, a project to bring out of retirement and maybe, just maybe, one more Badwater in me. I will be patient, be grateful. All is possible now. Believe, endure, have faith, show faith, show love. Thank you again, Lord, for the gift of this good news, it's more than a gift of hope. It's a gift of belief.

Frank continues to do all kinds of research. His latest quest: the best and most cutting-edge eating plan to follow. Increasing his red blood cell counts is key, so he tries any- and everything, including kidney meat and a mixture of spinach and beets every day. This helps, but the key part of his new routine has come about due to a well-timed encounter. As an enlightened Christian, Frank looks for angels in all forms, and this woman is most definitely heaven-sent. She does not have wings or a robe, but she was sent to him all the same, exactly on schedule. She is one of those valued collaborators and earth angels, and to this day Frank doesn't even know her name.

About five months earlier, just before Frank was officially diagnosed, a woman had bought one of his books after a keynote speech he'd delivered at an event, asked him to sign it, and chatted with him briefly. She was one of hundreds of people who had heard Frank speak that night.

When she sent him a private message later, he did not even remember meeting her. She did not want to alarm him, she wrote, but she also made this observation just a few days before he first got the devastating news about his condition:

I can see it in your face. There is something very wrong with you that you will soon learn, and it involves your blood. You should alkalize your body.

After years in the public eye, he was accustomed to people offering all kinds of dubious advice and left the message in his inbox, unanswered until after receiving the news about his condition. Then he quickly typed a thank-you and deleted her message, intent on getting back to dealing with his suddenly altered circumstances, but her message stayed with him.

Now he believes this woman had put her finger on something important, *alkalizing*. She had also given some specific dietary advice, and her message resonates; something is telling him to pay attention.

Already somewhat familiar with the concept of alkalizing the body, and sensing that this is a good course of action for him, Frank continues and dives into researching this further. Key to the program: citrus, particularly lemons. Though acidic, lemons metabolize and become alkaline upon entering the human body.

Frank doesn't just go for a teaspoon here and there. If a little is good, a lot is better, according to his life rules. It's somewhat of a joke in the family. For example, Nilsa appreciates but grows tired of his efforts to fix things around the house. A quick squirt of some WD-40 on a squeaky door might be all that's needed, yet Frank will spray the whole can on a single hinge. When she sees oil all over the door, streaking down, leaving a pool of the petroleum substance on the floor, Nilsa can only roll her eyes (again) because Frank feels the need to blow an entire can to fix one tiny squeak. (Unfortunately, "more" is a habit he can't seem to break.)

Frank's new task is to juice two large lemons each night by hand, as he's too eager to put them on a cutting board and use a squeezing machine. He just chops them in half and uses a hand squeezer, splattering juice all over the brand-new blue quartz countertops in their kitchen. He starts every morning by drinking lemon juice and water as they wake his brain up. Then the daily shake, which is a combination of a bunch of spinach, beets, bananas, blueberries, and blackberries mixed with black cherry juice, coconut water, collagen, protein, vitamin C, and wheatgrass powder. Push "liquify" and voila. During the day, he drinks a gallon of water to keep himself cleansed and hydrated.

Unfortunately, "more" is a habit
he can't seem to break.

Ultimately, the lemons are just one more practice he adds to his squeaky-clean living. Lots of people see the ripped jeans and the rock-star hairstyle and think it would be so great to party hard with Frank. But, hey, not so much. He swore off alcohol in his early twenties, steers away from caffeine, doesn't smoke, do drugs, gamble, or womanize, goes to bed at 9, and rises at 4. Given the routines he's followed most of his adult life, Frank is a lot less exciting than he looks.

$\mathcal{L}$AURA'S STORY

Apart from Mom and me, running is my father's one true love, the Badwater 135-mile ultramarathon his obsession. Of course I've always known dad loved to run. I watched him head out the door to run down Ocean Boulevard in front of our house for as long as I can remember.

The first time I went to one of Dad's Badwater ultramarathons, I was six and so excited. My grandmother took me out to Death Valley, California, explaining, "Your dad's running a really long race on the highway out in the desert. We'll find him as we drive along." I thought we would see him pretty quickly. I didn't realize Dad had signed up for several days in hell, also known as the world's toughest footrace.

We headed out in the car to catch up to my dad at mile 100 or so, and I sat in the backseat looking out the window, bewildered.

If you have not seen Death Valley, it's hard to imagine just what another world it is. It's almost post-apocalyptic, surface-of-the-moon-like, the kind of landscape I had never seen before. There was nothing and nobody out there as far as we could see, except that eventually, every so often, we would pass one of the runners. To me they looked like zombies. They were moving so slowly that it looked like a death march—and those were the ones who were still going! Others were stopped by the side of the road, throwing up, lying on the ground in agony with cramps, literally crawling, or passed out from heatstroke. I had never seen sights like this in my life. *This is what my dad is doing, too?* I wondered.

Laura at Badwater in 2005 (six years old)

When we finally recognized and approached my dad, he seemed to me to be in good spirits. He had already been running for more than 24 hours, and I figured he was feeling good because the end was in sight. It was only much later that I realized that his spirits were not high at all. His impressionable young daughter showing up so late in the race was the only thing that could have brought a smile to his face. At that point, most of the entrants were walking, at best, so they could be approached for a hug and quick talk. Dad really seemed OK, but only because he made a heroic effort to hide his true level of suffering.

The extent of that suffering I would see for myself only years later, as a teenager, when I joined Dad's crew, which was always led by Mom. The crew started with her, first and foremost. The Badwater organizers do not provide assistance during the race, and participants must provide their own crew to support them; follow them in a vehicle; bring them water, electrolyte drinks, food, sunscreen, body lube (to prevent chafing), cold towels, bandanas soaked in ice; and monitor their sodium, potassium, and magnesium levels—all the way down to keeping track of the color of their urine! Often, the crew needs to pick up their runner who, for a variety of reasons, simply cannot go on and has to drop out.

That first time I was a crew member, Mom and I were *crawling* along in the van. It was easily 120 degrees, and we were exhausted. Not as exhausted as Dad, obviously, but it had been a long haul, as we were 92 miles in. At that point Dad was forced to stop, and I became quite frantic when I realized his race was done.

"Mom! Can I finish for him? I know I could finish; I know it!"

"Honey, that's not how it works. Even if you wanted to and could actually make it, you're not registered for the race."

I burst into tears. "But why can't I do it? We have the same last name! I am an extension of him! Can't I just substitute in for Dad to the end? Please Mom, I know I can make it. Let me finish for him!"

I definitely had Dad's spirit of relentless forward motion.

"You just can't, Laurita, they would never allow it. And we must take care of Dad now. He needs us," Mom said. "Someday, you can run whatever race you want."

Mom was tired and worried about Dad's state of mind. And as I pulled myself together, she smiled at me, patted my shoulder, and said fondly, "You are your father's daughter, for sure."

I realized in that moment in the desert when I was 15 that I too could take my dad's "every single day" approach to my own life's adversities and watch it work its magic.

At the start of the sixth month since the diagnosis, Frank is now running 25 miles at a time. Slowly, but he's doing it. To Frank, the principles behind *every single day* are the easiest, though he realizes that to most people, they prove to be the hardest.

This idea of *every single day* has been recast in many ways over Frank's career as an author because it is such an integral part of his story and the life lessons he teaches. In all five of his nonfiction books, he wrote about living by these principles, only stated in different ways. If you've read any of his books, these chapter titles might sound familiar:

- "Take the Lunch Pail Approach While Answering Your Highest Calling" *(Make it BIG!)*
- "Make the Decision NOW to Put in the Time and Effort to Succeed" *(Maverick Approach)*
- "Close the Deal, Close the Loop" *(Burst This!)*
- "Get Off Your Knees and Start Walking" *(The Tap)*
- "Relentless Forward Motion" *(Aspire!)*

This idea of *every single day* has been recast in many ways over Frank's career as an author because it is such an integral part of his story and the life lessons he teaches.

As a young man, Frank didn't have an education, a degree, or a diploma beyond high school. When he started his career, he could not change a light bulb without breaking a couple of them first. It would be hard to find someone less technically inclined. He could barely read a set of plans, as he sees things in three dimensions instead of two, and he had to walk out to the jobsite to visually inspect progress versus what the plans say. He was terrible at skilled labor though great at unskilled labor. (Heck, just recently when he was stringing Christmas lights along the 72 flights of steps at the family's glass cabin in North Carolina, he actually stapled his hand to the rail because he was holding the staple gun backward.) In short, Frank was a linear, 1.8 GPA thinker who knew nothing more than to apply what he calls the Lunch Pail Approach. An homage to the hard-hatted, hardworking men and women on all his construction sites, the Lunch Pail Approach means nothing more than getting the job done every single day.

Frank has already been applying his *every single day* approach his whole life, so when it comes to his very first (and serious) health adversity he is conditioned and ready to do more of the same. Yes, it is easier for Frank than most because this has become his default mode. With nothing to fall back on, his only plan has always been to outwork everybody else. He started running ultramarathons because he saw a race, became intrigued, and thought: *All those people manage to run 135 miles through a desert? Why can't I?* It really is that simple.

* * *

If at this point you are tempted to close this book and use it as a door stopper because you don't want to do the hard work, know that the only part that's hard is starting then sticking to it. *Keep going.* Rewire that part of the brain, and it's not hard anymore. You have gotten through the hardest part of your adversity.

* * *

And now, after nearly a half a year of his new food regimen, the expensive blue quartz countertops near the kitchen sink show the wear and tear. The lemon juice that comes from Frank's frenzied lemon squeezing each night has eaten parts of the countertops away, disintegrating them. He doesn't mind. If this is not a visible sign of progress and a return to health, what is?

FRANK'S JOURNAL

I ran the farthest I have run in well over a year yesterday. I ran past Sunrise Boulevard for a total of 25 miles. In looking back over previous 25-mile times, I ran faster than last year when I was training for Badwater. Also, for the rest of the day I felt great! That's a good sign! I was not dragging by dinnertime. I look forward to a restful day of recovery after church. Thank you so much for all that you have done for me, Lord, especially my health over the last five months.

I'm preparing for what I will call my Yugo We-go Tour. I had this idea to take a huge risk and I'm going to do it, even if the country is mostly locked down due to COVID. I want to get away from my routine here, take to the road, and gather information along the way for my new book, *Aspire!* My goal is to eventually arrive in Death Valley, where I plan to unveil the cover and read a few paragraphs from the new book, then turn around and drive straight home.

Lord, allow me to enjoy and be fully engaged in the process. Allow the trip to be light and easy, as it should be fun. Finally, when I set out on tour in my Yugo, I pray that God blesses my little 0-to-60-in-never vehicle, that it makes it safely to my destination and back home.

FORGET A.D. AND TRY E.S.D.
(EVERY. SINGLE. DAY.) INSTEAD

There is only one action item for this chapter. Go back and review your notes from the Introduction through Chapter 3 and see how *far* you've come in overcoming your current adversity. Are you taking the actions at the end of each chapter? If so, they are surely paying off.

At the very beginning, when you first picked up this book and turned to page one, you could not imagine the progress you've now made. It was only aspirational to you back then. Now, putting your current adversity behind you is closer to becoming a reality.

P.S. Like you, Frank is human. *Every single day* is not literally *every day* without exception. Don't beat yourself up if you miss a few.

5

RISK IT

Defibrillate Yourself Back to Life

You'll never break free from that which constrains you unless you're willing to risk failure to test the strength of your perceived bondage.

By design, the previous chapter is methodical and deliberate. It's about pushing through routines that tempt you to quit due to the maddening mundaneness of the moment. Major breakthroughs are followed by minor meltdowns as your adversity tries to wrestle you to the ground, *again*. But you're always moving forward, relentlessly, slowly but surely. Considerable progress is being made. Yes, it is! So far, accomplishing "A-D-V-E" has removed you from that ledge where you had been barely hanging on by a thread.

And now it's time to take a risk and purposely smash into the guardrails created by your adversity to see if they're real or just an illusion. If they're real, you'll find out quickly. But if they're illusory, breaking through them will be easy, and you'll never be confined by the illusion, or this adversity, again.

* * *

During a less-than-stellar doctor's office visit one day, Frank learns that his red blood cell numbers are inexplicably getting worse again. He tells Dr. Garcia, "I don't want quantity of life, Doc. I want quality of life. I want to live now. I don't care too much about what happens when I'm 80. This condition must go away for good very soon."

* * *

If that is how you are feeling about your current "condition," then taking a risk at this juncture of facing your adversity is *exactly* what needs to happen. Right now is the time for a jump-start. A game-changing move.

* * *

Frank has a plan, one learned through experience.

As the speculative creator of high-end oceanfront real estate, he has lived through many business challenges and cycles over the course of his career, some quite serious. More than once he has flown so close to the sun that the skin on his face was blistering, ready to peel away as he was on the very brink of losing everything. The real estate crash and global recession of 2010 are perfect examples. Frank was extremely depressed over the state of his business. His anxiety level shot through the roof as he saw millions of dollars evaporate from his net worth every month. He was in real danger of losing his own oceanfront home of 25 years. Fortunately, Nilsa came up with an idea: to subdivide some of their property and offer three very desirable lots for sale while keeping the home where they raised Laura. Risky, yes, but with the cash generated from these sales, they could weather the storm.

As soon as the financial crisis was over and conditions leveled off, and with far less money in his bank account, Frank decided to venture out in his Yugo into the carnage left by the real estate Armageddon. He eventually spotted a modest, vacant ocean-view property with a falling-down FOR SALE sign in front of it. He bought it and started doing what he'd always loved, eventually creating the very first "micro-mansion."

Over the years, many times when business pressures threatened to overwhelm him, he has driven the 10 miles to the very first house he ever bought, way back in 1986, a tiny crack house in a dicey neighborhood. He would park in front of it and observe every detail, then remind himself, *You think your problems are so big and insurmountable now. Everything is falling apart with that $20 million house you're building. Well, look at this: There was a time you were delighted just to be in the real estate business, happy to flip crack houses!*

Revisiting the origin of the passion and purpose of being a real estate artist has never failed to help him past the immediate adversity. It assures him: With a little bit of risk, he will make it happen again.

Same thing with relationship issues. There have been times in his marriage when it didn't look like he and Nilsa would make it. During these tumultuous times when it seemed that he would lose his family, Frank has visited the church where he and Nilsa were married, sat in a pew, and remembered every detail of that joyful wedding day, the start of everything. *You idiot,* he berates himself, *you had it all and you messed it up. But you can bring back all the joy and love and hope you shared that day. Go fix it!* And so he does.

Now, to try to recapture the life Frank loved before his current health condition, it's time to take a huge risk again. To expedite the process and build on all the work he has done so far, there must be a moonshot. It's time to take out the defibrillator and give himself a shock back to life.

Frank is a let's-get-it-done beacon of optimism. A positive soul most always. In his quiet time, he has moments of doubt and despair like everyone else, but he is not one to indulge in feeling sorry for himself. But lately he's not feeling his usual upbeat and optimistic self, and he's sure been coddling himself. On a few nights a week his tears wet the pillow before he drifts off to sleep. As always, Nilsa is near, but inside he feels so alone. So, what does he do?

Well, he lifts his head up off the pillow one morning, jumps into his beloved Yugo, and drives it straight to the shop for a mechanical overhaul. Then he leaves it with a talented graphic vehicle wrap artist named Valerie

Landy for a custom job. He wants his Yugo to look rusty and abandoned, like it's been sitting out in a cornfield or a leaky old barn for a couple of decades. Valerie outdoes herself and gets every detail right. It has the look of peeling paint, exposed raw and corroded metal, all the way down to a rusty gas cap. The Yugo is like a four-wheeled version of Frank: not supposed to make it, battered, unique, lots of character. Most important: It still runs. It continues to endure.

Frank and his Yugo, together, can do this: He's going to drive across the country, solo, and reignite what it truly feels like to be alive. Where is he when he feels most engaged and fully his best self? Frank's "happy place"— ironically, Death Valley—lies almost 3,000 miles west of his home in Delray Beach. He plans stopovers in 22 cities along the way to gather information for his seventh book, *Aspire!* The risks are obvious and enormous. He is still taking chemo medicine. COVID rages throughout the country, and infection in his weakened condition would be the end. His car goes from zero to sixty in *never*. His wife is quite concerned about this trip. But Frank would rather die on the road than continue to live like this. Without these low times, he would not be risking it and taking off in his Yugo.

Yes, pills and lemon juice and health shakes and wigs, every single day. He will take it all with him and follow the plan, but this show's going on the road in a vehicle that is unlikely to make it to the local 7-Eleven, much less all the way to California and back. Yet Frank has complete faith that he will get there. He has no Plan B. He packs everything up and takes off on what he announces with great fanfare as a fact-finding prerelease tour for *Aspire!* The Yugo We-go Tour is so much more than a book tour or information-gathering trek. It is a journey for the redemption of his soul.

FRANK'S JOURNAL

Yesterday was a tough day. My red blood cell counts were off for the first time in several months for some unknown reason. I learned I may have to stay on Sprycel for another two years. While that probably won't wind up being the case, it will more than likely be 18 months. This was a huge blow to me, a dent to my spirit. I got emotional about it, even tearing up on the examination table as I sat in front of Dr. Garcia. I cried again before I went to bed. It was a sad and pathetic sight, crying all alone before I went to sleep. While I am still a strong individual, my weak moments seem to be closer to the surface than they've ever been before. I want the strong-minded Frank back.

I've prayed so hard for a breakthrough to that ever-elusive peace. I don't want to wake up one more time feeling the way I do after hearing results like I heard yesterday. This condition has tried to take parts of me that I used to own. I say tried, because it doesn't always succeed, but when it does, it slowly drains the beautiful person I am. I do try my best to stop these occurrences on my own, but I can't do it; I can't do anything without God's help.

This is where I am today: pleading and begging to be delivered from this back and forth. Restoration of my full health, a better version of myself. Therefore, I go to pick up my Yugo today with its new wrap. I must take this journey. I will be leaving for my Yugo We-go Tour this Wednesday. I need to build confidence and break this routine. Yes, I am nervous to leave the safety of home, but that's the very reason I am doing it. Yes,

COVID's out there, but here I am too comfortable and isolated. I am bordering on reclusive. I need my magnetism back. My confidence, my purpose. This is one risk worth taking, and I'm gonna do it.

ILSA'S STORY

I was not nearly as alarmed when Frank broached the idea of his long-haul Yugo tour as I was back when he decided to shuffle across Ocean Boulevard and he could barely walk. By the time he started scheming the Yugo We-go Tour, Frank was doing well. His numbers were, for the most part, all headed in the right direction, thanks to his—our—diligence. I was a big part of that diligence, tending to him every day in every way possible, my "tool" bag always at my side.

Frank was determined to go on this excursion by himself, which meant I would no longer have any control over his recovery. But I had to step back from that desire, immediately, because I knew this trip would be the best and most necessary part of his recovery. I understood his mindset well enough to know that this was something he needed to do for himself and by himself. He was certainly doing his part when it came to the physical side of getting well: swallowing those hated pills, going along with Dr. Garcia (for the most part), the health shakes, the lemon juice, the gallon of water daily, the exercise routine and so on. I understood that this was a mental healing journey he needed to take.

"Don't die or I'll kill you!"

Still, it was so hard to say good-bye to him the day he took off. I grabbed his face, one hand on each cheek, to really look deeply into his eyes before our kiss good-bye. *After all this progress we've made, he better take good care of himself, or I will kill him!* That was my thought as the car disappeared down Ocean Boulevard. Laura could see how wrenching this parting was for me and tried to reassure me.

"He's going to be fine, Mom. He's Dad. He's always going to be fine." She put her arm around me, and we walked back into the suddenly quiet house.

There was certainly a void the first several nights, and I didn't quite know what to do with myself. Frank and I were so tightly bound during the recovery months that it was very strange to now be apart. I fretted: *I hope he can find his organic fruits. Did he remember to take his lucky T-shirt?* There were endless things for me to wonder and worry about. Then I got ahold of myself. I had to let this kind of thinking go and again, relinquish any idea of control. I reminded myself that Frank would certainly manage to get whatever he needed on the road. Somehow. If there's one thing I knew about my husband, one of his best traits, is that he is very resourceful.

Ostensibly and publicly, the Yugo We-go Tour is research for Frank's upcoming book, *Aspire!,* in which he writes about transforming one's own reality. He stops in numerous cities to speak to all kinds of people about their own day-to-day realities. Their hopes, their dreams, their needs, what they would most like to alter in their life. He meets with such a wide cross-section of Americana, from down-and-out residents of homeless shelters on the outskirts of Amarillo to guests at a five-star hotel in Aspen. He baffles patrons in a famous New Orleans bar by ordering lemon juice instead of what they assumed he would order (Jack Daniels or something).

Frank is humbled by the kindness of strangers, the deep-seated secrets and confidences shared with him, the thoughtful answers to questions he poses about legacies and guardian angels. The research could not be more valuable. Just as important: the sights, the sounds, the smells, the tastes. All of this allows Frank to remember what it feels like to live without this condition.

This trip is about so much more than just gathering information for *Aspire!* As Frank nears his destination, he realizes that, in essence, he has been interviewing himself over the thousands of miles. He is learning, shifting, and growing—and he comes to a decision, albeit minor in the scheme of things.

In Las Vegas, Frank visits a hair salon in one of the fancy hotels on the Strip. He has been making the wigs work for months as his hair has been coming back in, at first thin and patchy, and more recently showing some potential for looking presentable again. He's tired of the wigs and their upkeep, which takes a lot of time to make the hair look like his own. He arrives at the salon and gets a keratin treatment on his own natural locks.

It really works, too: looking in the mirror, he sees that his hair looks sleek, shiny, and much longer and thicker than usual. He looks almost normal again, back to his old self. It's good enough! He would much rather have people look at his posts and say, "What a terrible short haircut on him!" as opposed to, "What the hell is he wearing on his head?"

And just like that, Frank changes his plan. He decides that he will not resign himself to wearing a hairpiece or wig any longer as he strives for complete molecular remission. He packs up the wigs and never looks back. He is becoming free in many ways.

And then it's September 18, just 10 days after he left home, and Frank and his (t)rusty Yugo roll into Death Valley! Frank snaps a photo of himself at the entrance to Death Valley National Park, and the look on his face says it all. He has done it, returned to the place he loves the most, the scene of seven hard-won Badwater personal victories, as well as many other agonizing attempts to finish the race. This journey has allowed Frank to revive something that his condition has caused to lay dormant inside him: his very essence, his aura. This rebirth wouldn't have happened without taking this risk.

Frank's Yugo miracle: Delray to Death Valley—3,000 miles!

Arriving safely at Badwater Basin, soaking in the familiar atmosphere of the place where Frank has enjoyed his greatest trials and triumphs is a cathartic, life-enhancing, golden moment. But Frank still has a long journey ahead, all the way back home. What has he learned from being out there? That this journey is a necessary step in getting through this adversity.

FRANK'S SOCIAL MEDIA POST

(Sept. 18, 2020)

For many, this won't mean much. For others it will mean something. For me and my family, today means everything. A little over six months ago I had a life-threatening illness and didn't leave my own room for two weeks. I will never forget how Nilsa sat in that chair by our bed for weeks as I slept, watching over me, making sure my chest was still rising and falling. With Nilsa and Laura's love and care, I have slowly crawled back into my life.

At my lowest points, my thoughts and aspirations often drifted to my favorite place, Death Valley National Park, and the Badwater ultramarathon. Would I ever go back? Well, just look at the smile on my face in these pictures. Back at my summer desert home and able to run 20 miles up and down Towne Pass in the heat of the day. The other pictures are from landmarks along the Badwater racecourse. On top of all that, my Yugo made all 2,998 miles from Florida to that white line between hell and heaven!

It took relentless forward motion, not only through the miles in my tiny Yugo, but with my condition, to get here, to today, alive. But I reached my destination! Where I sit today, and after what I've learned from interviewing many along the way, I am so grateful to God for gifting me with the joy I experienced crossing into Death Valley.

*N*ILSA'S STORY

When you're deeply connected to your partner, you feel their joy, and it becomes your joy as well. I could not have been happier for my husband when he reached his destination.

Frank was great about staying in touch, sending updates, photos, calling, and texting. When he arrived safely in Death Valley, I received a photo of him at the park entrance with that truly genuine smile on his face—one from his gut, one I hadn't seen for a long time. He looked so happy that I broke down crying, because I knew he was in the one place he loves the most and was doing exactly what he wanted to do where he mentally and physically wanted to be. This place would give him the emotional returns he needed.

> When he arrived safely in Death Valley, I received a photo of him at the park entrance with that truly genuine smile on his face— one from his gut, one I hadn't seen for a long time.

I was also delighted that he took off the wig for good. It was such a big deal, those wigs; it caused a lot of stress when they didn't fit right, look right, were uncomfortable. It was an enormous relief to us both to finally put them aside for the last time. Frank's trip was a true coming-out journey in many ways. One I would soon join!

You have followed Professor Frank all this way. Now it's time to man up, woman up, human up, and risk it yourself.

It is never easy to take a substantial risk. During adversity we let our cautious, rational minds run the show and no longer listen to the urgings of the heart and soul to "Go for it!" But there comes a point during efforts to move past adversity when at least a few people will be shaking their heads and asking, "What in the world are you thinking?" If that doesn't happen, you are playing way too small.

During adversity we let our cautious, rational minds run the show and no longer listen to the urgings of the heart and soul to "Go for it!"

Yes, you have read an entire chapter saying how methodical your *every single day* must be, but taking your own personal moonshot involves risks. The progress that you have made has been incremental, two steps forward, 1.99 steps back, inching along, and now it's time to shake off being so methodical. Your goal: to physically take yourself to a place where you feel most alive and happy. Your purpose: to viscerally remind yourself in the proper setting that your life is going to be *better* than it was when you were there before, when you were healthy, or your business was thriving, or your relationship still inspired you both, whatever the case may be.

This seismic shift in routine is necessary to fast-track you to the next stage. This is the next necessary pursuit if you want to move beyond your adversity as quickly as possible. Yes, you are grinding it out every single day, and that is all to the good. No doubt you are reaping some rewards. But it's time to shake things up in the most dramatic way possible. A "shock run" for someone who regularly logs six miles would not be defined as running seven miles; it would be running 12. To shock the mind to show you what you are truly capable of, it's time for your own personal version of a shock run.

To truly overcome your own adversity, you should revisit a place where you were most at peace before your current "situation," whatever it may be. Reconnect to a time, place, or person where this pall was not even a shadow of your reality.

The purpose of this "risk it" exercise is to make a quantum break from the reality that your adversity has created and for you to reignite a better, more enlightened version of yourself.

Oprah Winfrey, among her many other accomplishments, coined a popular phrase, the "aha moment," which officially entered the *Merriam-Webster English Dictionary* in 2012. At the time, she said, "You can't have an 'aha' unless you already knew it. So, the aha is the remembering of what you already knew, articulated in a way to resonate with your own truth."

Here, through the pursuit of your own "aha moment" you can instinctively remind yourself that there is no need for a new normal, only a more frequent extraordinary.

What if you can't afford to take off like Frank did? You don't have to disappear for weeks to a place that made you feel most alive and most joyous—like a childhood home, a camp setting, a distant wilderness, or beach somewhere. If your healing "aha" place is far away, and you can afford it, of course invest in this adversity-busting experience. But if you can't afford that, think of a location that is within 100 miles of where you live (but not at home). Go there alone with a collection of things that evoke healing energy: your favorite books, special stones or beads, religious or other spiritual mementos, letters, journals, videos, photos, etc.—and bring nothing associated with your current adversity unless it's absolutely necessary.

Spend at least a few days alone, preferably involving some forms of nature, with this healing energy. An exception would be visiting a friend or spiritual advisor who you have not involved in your current adversity, but do this only after spending some time alone.

The purpose of this "risk it" exercise is to make a quantum break from the reality that your adversity has created and for you to reignite a better, more enlightened version of yourself.

ILSA'S STORY

I wanted Frank to be free to do what he wanted on his own schedule, to wander where he would. He was wonderful about sharing his experience. But on his return trip to Florida, he was eager to revisit several of the places he had stopped and share them with me. So I got on a plane to Colorado, where he greeted me with flowers and a lovely dinner, and we stayed in Manitou Springs for a couple of days. Then back on the road, the two of us in that little sputtering car. Truly, I just prayed it would get us home in one piece. I was amazed it had made it to Death Valley in the first place.

The Midwest plains went on forever, endless, mile after mile of flat, monotonous landscape. It felt as remote as the desert. Very few people or other cars, but huge farms everywhere. The pungent smell of cow manure permeated the Yugo for days. I was a bit concerned that this portion of the trip would drive Frank crazy, because normally he would be fidgeting and antsy on such a long, dull drive through the unvarying countryside. Yet there was something incredibly beautiful about this expanse of peaceful land, going hours without another soul in sight. So simple and elemental, a vista we were not used to seeing.

This led to plenty of time to catch up and reconnect. Deep conversations, where I got to hear all his thoughts and stories from the tour. We had the rare opportunity of time together with zero diversions. I could see a difference in him immediately. Frank was much more of his "old" self, but a better version. That wig was gone, and his energy was coming back. More important, his confidence had returned. With his own hair growing, he felt better going out in public, and he had that huge achievement, a 3,000-mile cross-country trek on his own, under his belt. A better Frank was sitting beside me in that little car.

FRANK'S JOURNAL

(Oct. 2, 2020)

It's now 23 days since I left on the Yugo We-go Tour, and it's over. I woke up in my own bed this morning. I want to devote this journal to thanking you, God, for giving me the experience of the Yugo We-go Tour. The places I stopped included Delray, Orlando, Tallahassee, Mobile, New Orleans, Dallas, Amarillo, Albuquerque, Sedona, Flagstaff, Las Vegas, Death Valley, Salt Lake City, Richfield, Aspen, Manitou Springs, Dodge City, Tulsa, Little Rock, Memphis, Atlanta, Ocoee, and back to Delray.

I still can't believe the Yugo made it all that way. I am so thankful that God allowed my little car to log 6,288.7 miles without a problem! And I was spared from catching any kind of illness. The miles were safe ones. Meeting the beautiful people along the way, being joined by Nilsa on the way back for the last 2,000 miles . . .

Above all, thank you, Lord, for returning me to health through this experience. As I lie here in the same bed where I was close to death only seven months ago, I know that I could never have imagined the gifts that would present themselves by taking this huge risk.

DARE TO RISK IT

Schedule your own "risk it" adventure that will allow you to experience the peace and joy you had before your adversity. Your objective upon returning is not to have some new normal, but a more frequent extraordinary. Schedule this within one week of reading this chapter or you probably won't do it! Think of it as a personal retreat where you allow your mind to move beyond focusing on the suffering that your adversity is causing you.

P.S. It's important that you finish this book before you undertake your "risk it" experience, but at least schedule it now. By finishing *Adversitology*, you will get the most out of your "risk it" adventure, and its results will be long-lasting and far more impactful.

Of course, if you are reading this book and aren't currently experiencing any form of adversity, you can wait to schedule your "risk it" adventure. But why? You will always receive a great benefit from taking a risk, whether through adversity or just in everyday life.

Think of it as a personal retreat where you allow your mind to move beyond focusing on the suffering that your adversity is causing you.

6

SAVOR EVERYTHING. CLING TO NOTHING.

Live Now Because Living Then Won't Be Any Better

Fireworks are exploding, the band is playing, and confetti is raining down. You've come so far in this quest to accept, manage, and move past whatever adversity is affecting you. The countdown to liberation is approaching. This adversity is nearly behind you!

Now a good 9+ months into his recovery, Frank has completed his triumphant cross-country Yugo tour and is about 75 percent finished with writing *Aspire!* His blood tests are looking good. He has lowered the dosages of his chemo medicine. He's running 25 miles in one go. Even his hair is nearly back to normal! He is making fantastic progress.

What he does not realize is how he is clinging to this progress in a most unhealthy way. Any backsliding—running times slower than usual, a less-than-favorable result on his bloodwork, an unexpected drop in energy or rise in pain—like the flip of a switch, it sends his emotions in the wrong direction. Why the mercurial existence? Why such sensitivity to these seemingly minor setbacks? The lesson, which is key to enjoying life in good times as well as periods of adversity, is learning how to let go of the attachments we cling to so desperately. Nothing could come harder for Frank.

Of all the letters in the A-D-V-E-R-S-I-T-Y plan, he struggles the most with S. Many others may stumble with "Acceptance" because of denial, "Disidentify" because of association, "Violate Fate" because of wanting to adhere to other's rules, "Every. Single. Day." because of boredom and commitment difficulties, and "Risk It" because of fear. Most of these come easily for Frank, but not "Savor Everything. Cling to Nothing." His toughest adversary shows its ugly head now, toward the end of the process, just as the finish line is in sight.

FRANK'S JOURNAL

(A PROPHETIC ENTRY)

Answer honestly: What would change, what would be different, if I were told today that I am completely free of this condition? Well, at first I would naturally be extremely grateful, probably tearful. I would get on my knees and thank God for curing me. I would immediately stop taking all medicines, and I would wait for my energy levels to rise again—to even higher than they were before this happened.

So that's probably how I would react, but what in my life would have actually changed in, say, three months after I was pronounced "cured"? Would things really be much different than they are right now? Would I be happier inside and outside and discover more joy around myself? While I can't answer that for sure, getting my energy back would certainly be nice. Beyond that, I'm not too sure much at all would be different than it is right this very moment. Think about that!

For decades, I have tied my happiness to future events: a sale of one of our oceanfront mansions, a certain net worth, completion of the next masterpiece or building a Caring House village in Haiti or finishing another successful Badwater run or concluding a book tour. I promise myself that I will be satisfied and happy when these things happen, the latest being told "You're cured." If I'm going to be honest, I know I will become overly attached to the feeling I get when I hear those magic words. I also know for sure that something else will soon take the place of this current condition as the next Everest I need to climb.

There's nothing that I can write down to change that reaction; the only thing that will curb this tendency is awareness—and rewiring and redirecting my thoughts. I need to believe that this great result has already occurred, and that while I will savor it and accept it gratefully, I will not cling to that elusive high that comes from those feelings.

Because, you know what, Frank? Get real. You might never get better! What you have right here, right now is all there really is—you can't put off living now because you perceive that living then will be better!

$\mathcal{L}$AURA'S STORY

I definitely have the adrenaline-seeking, love for excitement, impulsive gene. Thanks, Dad! I became a runner in high school, mostly doing 5Ks, which is about three miles. After a few of those, I understood much better what running 135 miles involved for him. The training, the gym workouts, the mindset, the equipment. For my dad, nearly every day during "Badwater season" revolved around the annual Death Valley race. His intense focus was formidable.

After watching him traverse the desert, a marathon sure seemed easy enough. What's 26 miles? It truly seemed doable. As long as my body didn't give out, my will would push me over the finish line, even walking if I had to. On a whim in my junior year of college, I entered the lottery for the New York City Marathon. It was an item on my bucket list, and somehow I got in on my very first try. I was so busy at school that I didn't really have time for formal training and was able to squeeze in only a couple of 3-mile runs before the marathon, so I decided just to show up and have a good time.

Talk about ignorance being bliss. Finishing 26 miles was grueling, of course. But I never had a doubt that I would get through it. I told myself it was four hours of running; I knew I could force myself to the finish line. Overall, I had an exciting time. Every muscle in my body hurt afterward, but my mood was euphoric, and I recovered quickly. It was a huge achievement! It helped me so much in my life: going forward with confidence. I truly realized what my will could do if I made a choice to make it happen.

Laura's New York City Marathon

Dad could not believe that my longest training run was only 3 miles, which he called insanity. Who just shows up to run a marathon? Most participants follow an intense program to prepare, going on progressively longer runs of around 18 to 22 miles. For me, it was 3?! He was sure I had managed to finish only because I had the proper mindset and youth on my side. I have to agree.

But I'll add that there is no question I had my own attachment to this kind of impulsive, thrill-seeking act. Growing up, I had observed firsthand and up close how this trait affected my dad's life. I saw times when this worked for him very well, just as this marathon had for me—and also times when it was not so great. I knew these types of attachments were something I had to keep an eye on in myself.

It is all for the best that Frank never joined a band and became a literal rock star. The adulation, the travel, the women, the high of being onstage in front of cheering crowds—oh, how he would be *very* good at that. And how hard he would chase that sensation for the rest of his life. He completely relates to the performers who retire from the stage after decades of touring and then don't know what to do with themselves. These "retirees" often get into trouble because there are no longer enough extreme highs. Frank relates all too well to this type of thrill-seeking. Like a rat in a lab experiment, he will keep hitting that electrified bar to keep the feeling going.

Frank and his therapist agree: He is addicted to excitement.

Like a rat in a lab experiment, he will keep hitting that electrified bar to keep the feeling going.

So naturally, when it's time to promote his new book, he comes up with his most outrageous, most dangerous, most elaborate stunt yet. After deciding against revealing the book cover while he was in Death Valley, everything about *Aspire!* is still under a shroud of secrecy. Frank has not divulged the title, theme, or its cover. He has said only that in this seventh book he will focus for the first time on mindset, and that's all the information the public has. He ponders how best to reveal its message: *We're going to aspire to break through and create our own reality!*

In keeping with his motto, *go bigger than anyone else,* he decides to light himself on fire and race a motorcycle through an enormous flaming image of his new book cover. (You can see this stunt on Frank's YouTube channel.) Such an elaborate show is more than some shallow tribute to Frank's ego, though. For sure he enjoys the spotlight and wowing a crowd, but mainly he wants the people gathered for this spectacle to see a guy who worked through his fear, took a big risk, and triumphs in the end.

He has quite a bit of trepidation as the event starts to come together. For one thing, it's been years since he's ridden a motorcycle.

But if Frank is going to do this, he's going to do it right. He works with a stunt team for weeks to prepare, even rehearsing the flaming inferno in a deserted parking lot in the middle of the night. He secures the various zoning permissions required to close down Main Street in his hometown of Delray Beach, Florida. He hires firefighters to monitor the flames and local cops for security on the street for the entire night. He is abuzz with anticipation, running around making endless detailed preparations for this once-in-a-lifetime book reveal extravaganza. In the moment, he is hardly keen on the principle of savoring everything, clinging to nothing.

Frank does not drink alcohol in large part because he doesn't like to dull his natural feelings or come down in any way. He is all about enhancing and amplifying. If a little excitement is good, then a lot is waaay better. That's how he's lived for 50-plus years, anyway. He is an athlete: a guy who runs, works out religiously, eats mostly fresh and whole foods, and drinks a gallon of water a day. But Frank does have a small cache of prescription drugs: Adderall, to stay awake and on his feet during his multiday training runs, and a handful of powerful painkillers, prescribed over the years to treat his many debilitating injuries, particularly his blown-out knees.

For someone like Frank who lives such a clean life, the Adderall, which is simply a form of speed, can hit like a freight train, like a shot of cocaine. Same goes for opiates, the painkillers. That is why the drugs are safely in their bottles in a box in Nilsa's dresser, rarely if ever seen, much less used.

Drugs are not a regular part of their life. Which makes what he does next pretty bewildering.

The filming of the big book reveal event for *Aspire!* comes off just as Frank imagines. Nope, even better! Spectators line both sides of Main Street in the predawn hours. Huge spotlights shine on the action. As the two-story-high, brightly colored banner of the book cover unfurls, Frank sits atop a shiny orange Harley-Davidson motorcycle while a stuntman applies fire-accelerator all over the back of his jean jacket and helmet with a brush.

"Let's fire up this reality and aspire to break through it! Together!" Frank urges the crowd.

The helmet goes on, the stuntman lights up his back in flames, and he pegs the throttle.

Another thrill-induced high that wasn't enough

The various police cars have their lights flashing. Onlookers watch with bated breath from darkened storefronts as Frank screams down the street with his clothes ablaze, makes a skidding turn around the last cop car and races balls to the wall at his flaming target. He bursts through to wild cheers, then comes to a halt, where he is quickly doused with multiple fire extinguishers.

Amid the swirl of smoke, Frank removes his helmet, and in one take delivers his lines to camera, ending with, "Well, that was hot. Literally!"

His dangerous stunt has gone off without a hitch, and crystalline-pure adrenaline is still coursing through his veins.

Lighting himself ablaze and busting his motorcycle through that raging wall of fire was so thrilling that now he feels as if he simply cannot let the feeling end. So when he and Nilsa arrive home—and without her knowledge—he pulls out his box of pills and opens it. Frank has been performing on Main Street all night, and it is approaching dawn as he pops a few pills in a bid to prolong the thrill. Then what? He never goes to sleep at all that day, which is actually a regular, mundane Sunday of working, going to church, and puttering around the house. There is also time for some serious soul-searching. *WTF?!*

FRANK'S JOURNAL

Yesterday between 3 and 6 a.m. we shot the video on Main Street for the reveal of my seventh book. It was so much fun! That guy in flames is who I am—or at least a big part of who I've been for my entire life. The stunt was thrilling and went off without a single flaw. I'd put it in the top 10 experiences I've ever had, and I've had a bunch. They say when you get older there are so few firsts remaining in life. Well, it was nice to have a first like this!

I will certainly relive this moment for days. There could be times it's overshadowed by my apparent need to continue to amplify the experience by taking those pills like I did last night. Yes, after the thrilling stunt, I took an Adderall and two pain pills the minute I was safely back at home. I confessed to Nilsa that I had done so, and she understood what had happened: I hadn't wanted the feeling to end.

By trying to hang on to the feeling artificially, I didn't really savor it properly. As I sat there at 6:55 a.m., empty pillbox in hand, I realized that I am tired of amplifying my life. I want to be satisfied with what I experience and then move on. I devote too much ink to this shit when I should be writing more about my latest once-in-a-lifetime experience!

I am tired of amplifying my life.

At my age I scripted, wrote, directed, and starred in a stunt where I rode a motorcycle through a burning image of my seventh book (a cover I also designed). I did all this while being lit on fire and delivering lines to a camera in one take with no do-overs. Why in God's name isn't this enough?

This, of course, is the million-dollar question.

———◦———

Americans have always identified with achievers. Striving is in the national DNA. Many have the tendency to aspire high, and quite a few have the grit and drive to set personal goals and reach them. Sure, getting there is hard, but once you are hired for that job, marry that person, hit that ideal weight, have that child, achieve that promotion, make however many dollars a year, then life will really begin.

What most of the people who attain any lofty goal don't realize is that achieving that milestone will not give them more than a few moments of happiness or joy. These achievements offer only a temporary thrill, a pleasure that initially grows in intensity then turns into pain should you lose the milestone or boredom if you keep it.

Any achievement, and the feeling it gives you, can grow into an attachment. Almost every negative emotion you experience (anxiety, depression, fear, jealousy, anger, boredom, etc.) is directly tied to some form of attachment. So now it's on to the next thing, because once you possess something, it's rarely enough to satisfy you.

**These achievements offer only a temporary thrill,
a pleasure that initially grows in intensity
then turns into pain should you lose the
milestone or boredom if you keep it.**

This attachment "hamster wheel" is no way to go through life. It's like having a heroin needle routinely stuck into your vein, something Frank has done, only figuratively, for most of his adult life.

* * *

The pill incident after his book launch really jolts Frank. His personal attachment to the need for excitement and constant stimulation can no longer be ignored. He has crossed a dangerous red line, and he is sick and tired of living this way. Perhaps he's just getting older, perhaps his condition has taken a toll, but he simply is starting to run out of the energy such a lifestyle requires. After decades of pushing things too hard, this is his opportunity to strip himself (as well as his loved ones and therapist) of the long-held certainty that he is hardwired as an adrenaline junkie and thrill-seeker. There is a better way to live.

As is his habit, Frank dives into research, reading psychology books and scientific journals about the nature of attachment.

* * *

At the most basic level, humans learn early on to form attachments. It's important for babies to attach to their caregivers, and they can even become quite attached to certain toys or foods. It all starts when we humans encounter something that gives us pleasure. As adults, objects or experiences like getting a new car, going on an exciting date, winning big in Vegas, moving into a dream home, or visiting that beautiful (and IG-worthy) tropical vacation spot absolutely bring on a sense of well-being. The problem comes with the need to repeat this gratifying sensation, followed by the belief and growing conviction that you cannot be happy without more. It's a maddening cycle that becomes amplified only when dealing with adversity.

Many of us know someone who has faced dreadful adversity—a death in the family, debilitating financial setbacks, a terminal illness—who nonetheless remain serene and calm throughout every excruciating moment. These people get it.

* * *

Frank is not yet a person who has truly mastered nonattachment and savors every moment, though he has caught brief glimpses of what this way of life holds. He can taste the possibilities. He turns to enlightened teachings once again, starting with a book by Barbara O'Brien.

"We 'attach' to things out of a sense of incompleteness and neediness," he reads. No doubt about that one. In another insightful passage, Frank reads, "Chasing blissful states can itself become a form of desire and attachment, and the path toward enlightenment is to surrender clinging and desire." And there it is in a nutshell.

Anthony de Mello also describes the pattern: "Once again the weary cycle: attraction, pleasure, attachment, fulfillment, satisfaction, boredom."

$\mathcal{L}$AURA'S STORY

I love New York City, a place where every single day is an adventure and you have no idea what you'll see or receive at any given moment. Just living in the city is a shot of adrenaline. Heading out on a Friday night, my pulse beats a bit faster, because I know that literally anything is possible here. I live for this feeling of joyous anticipation. It's no doubt a big part of why I was so eager to move here after college.

Still, New York City is, as advertised, tough. I certainly learned here what it's like to have things not work out as I hoped and expected them to. For example, I was rejected for countless jobs over the past few years. That was humbling and a bit of a shock for someone who had always been a high achiever. I hadn't faced many losses or defeats in my life until I moved here, and that changed in a hurry.

To keep going, my mindset had to change. I was forced to learn not to become attached to a dream outcome for any of the many, many jobs I applied for, some of which I was sure would be perfect for me. These employers didn't really know me. In most cases they were simply reviewing a sheet of paper (and discarding it). I knew I had to keep on applying, getting out there, networking, and have faith that something good, employment-wise, would eventually happen. Someday, hopefully sooner rather than later. Rejection is hard on everyone. Much was required: self-care, self-soothing, and plenty of pep talks with the mirror.

I may be fortunate to have learned how to apply patience early in my life, but this attribute has never been my dad's strong suit. This worried me as a daughter who observed him while he was fighting his health condition. He pushed himself so hard so often when, really, he needed to rest. I was concerned he was affecting his recovery and not in the way he intended. His body was already beating him up, and I wished that just once he would allow himself grace, time, and acceptance to fully heal.

One day, he came staggering inside after an extended session in his sauna followed by lying in the hot sun for 30 minutes afterward. I could immediately see that something was wrong. His pupils were dilated and he was sweating profusely, clearly on the verge of heatstroke or something. Once again, he had pushed himself too far, too fast, and I was worried. But immediately on the heels of my initial reaction came the thought, *This is really going to stress Mom out, and she doesn't need to deal with this on top of everything else.*

This is the domino effect on families when it comes to attaching too much to outcomes. Pushing yourself with a monomaniacal focus to reach a goal can be good, but sometimes it hurts. Sometimes, it leaves a mess that others must clean up. Family can get hurt over these attachments, which is something that's always been on my mind as I've watched my father all my life. My mom and I have both been affected.

All those ultramarathons at Badwater, for example: my dad truly lives for them. But my mom was always a key part of his successes. She was on his crew all 12 times he raced there, and it was grueling for her physically on top of her worries about him.

Dad was also so attached to the success of all his books, for another example. Only he would choose to release three books in three different genres on the same day! We were always proud of his achievements—athletic, business, charity endeavors, literary—but sometimes he took things a little too far. His novel *The Other Thief* was not an enjoyable book for my mom or me and many of our friends, as it was a little too personally revealing and it pained us to read those words. Dad meant no harm, but there was no deterring his attachment to the excitement of this new genre, this new project.

To see that sometimes Dad's focus was not always necessarily on those who loved him and supported him in every endeavor was a cautionary lesson. Fortunately, I learned early on how to tame this in myself. My mother's genes and influence no doubt helped. I realize it is important to control some of these wilder impulses. I might have to stop and consider how they will affect my loved ones. And I'll admit that this is not always easy when, at my core, I am my father's daughter!

> ## To see that sometimes Dad's focus was not always necessarily on those who loved him and supported him in every endeavor was a cautionary lesson.

Frank begins to accept and practice the "savor everything, cling to nothing" mindset. He has come a long way and is becoming a different man in this adversity-filled time. Living the life of a Renaissance man is a complex blessing. His life will always be a mosaic; he will likely always struggle to tame his mercurial side. Practicing nonattachment has not been a straightforward, easy path, but the results are impressive. Not that he's currently sitting in the lotus position atop a mountain in Tibet, but he has certainly managed to become somewhat enlightened. An enthusiastic convert, he wants everyone to know what it feels like not to cling to this kind of progress, to get off that wheel, to savor peak experiences—yes, they make life delightful—and not attach.

A more enlightened dad with his little girl!

FRANK'S JOURNAL

Working out this morning, I slipped on my treadmill and really hurt myself, which required a quick trip to the ER. But I have been able, in the short time since the accident this morning, not to attach to my immediate thoughts of, *Oh, our New Year's trip is going to be ruined because now I can't get on a plane to Colorado,* and *My speaking event tomorrow night! I can't miss it!*

Instead, I snapped a selfie on my brand-new crutches. Then I sent it to the event host with a message that said, "Hey, guys, I messed up. Sorry I can't make it tomorrow." I settled in, not for the showstopping keynote I had planned, but a quieter weekend recovering at home.

The acceptance wasn't immediate. I did tear up this morning after it all happened. It really hurt, but not as much as the realization that I may truly be at the end of my running career. My knees are completely destroyed, and I am looking at a knee replacement, maybe soon. But instead of lamenting my fate and attaching to memories of the glory days competing at Badwater, I disidentified with the pain and what this injury did to all my plans. I will make an appointment soon with a knee surgeon, and whatever he recommends, I'll consider. Just like that.

I'm going with it.

None of this would have happened without my condition and what it taught me. This could really be the end of running for me. I may not be able to do it anymore. I asked myself: *What would you rather have, Frank? Would you rather have your condition come raging back and be able to run, or would you rather be condition-free and not able to run?*

Wait a minute. I was playing the attachment game again. The answer is neither and both at the same time!

I couldn't immediately call on my very own and very new philosophy after a fall from the treadmill and the realization that my running career may be over. My reaction wasn't automatic, still not my default, but within an hour it was happening, and it worked to settle my mind and restore some peace.

———

You may not find this step difficult at all, as not everyone has an excitement-seeking gene or disposition. However, most everybody clings to or attaches to certain things that no longer serve them. Think about what you are most attached to. You have no doubt encountered many experiences that give you pleasure, which brought on the desire to keep that feeling going. Naturally, you want to repeat that gratifying sensation, leading to the conviction that you cannot be happy without that person, object, or success that you previously enjoyed. Just be aware that it can become a slippery slope of endless longing and chasing.

Pleasure = happiness is an incorrect equation for life satisfaction. Peak moments are wonderful, but holding onto them, not so much. Excitement and thrills are not happiness. True happiness comes from within, and it is uncaused and unaffected by outside events.

The pursuit and attainment of material things will provide two things in all the abundance you can imagine: relief and comfort. But notice what's missing: uncaused joy and happiness.

And finally: If you wonder whether you have become enlightened, it is almost certain you have not.

SAVOR THIS
(BUT DON'T CLING TO IT)

With nonattachment there is no action, just awareness and understanding. You must see with unflinching clarity this simple and shattering truth: Contrary to what your culture and religion may have taught you, nothing, absolutely nothing, can make you happy. Nothing outside of you can bring you lasting joy. Don't settle for reform when what is needed is revolt.

7

I AM NOT ALONE

You Don't Need to Face Your Adversity Alone

Move forward with faith, which is "being sure of what you hope for and certain of what you do not see." (Hebrews 11:1)

The quote above is from the Bible, but the idea could just as easily have come from the Quran, ancient birch-bark Buddhist scrolls, or a fortune cookie from your favorite Chinese restaurant. This aspirational passage about the power of faith is equally applicable to *everyone,* no matter their religious persuasion (if they even have one) or who or what they put their faith in.

Note: If any part of this chapter triggers judgement, prejudice, or even the slightest feeling of unease, you are invited to skip ahead to the next one, "Time to Terminate." If you would prefer not to read about or share in this exploration of one journey of faith during a near-death health adversity, of course that's your prerogative, and the A-D-V-E-R-S-I-T-Y plan will certainly still work wonders. Just look at how much help it's been so far!

In the pages ahead, you can read about one man's experiences, circumstances in his life that point to the reliance on faith as examples, and if you choose to take something from them, that's great!

* * *

The New Testament definition of faith is one of Frank's go-to verses, both to recite and to live by. When he presents it in keynote speeches, Hindus, Muslims, Jews, Buddhists, and, yes, even agnostics and atheists in the audience say it resonates. But Frank has never been one to preach, evangelize, pound on the pulpit, or shove the Bible down anyone's throat. He respects the reality that some people may have no desire to hear that he attributes a large part of his ability to endure adversity to his unshakeable conviction that he is not alone, no matter the battle.

If Jesus were here in our world today and wearing studded, ripped jeans with colorful jackets, and he had long purple hair and a Yugo, how would he act? What would he do? That's the filter through which Frank approaches nearly every single day of his life. He has always preferred to evangelize with action, not words.

If Jesus were here in our world today and wearing studded, ripped jeans with colorful jackets, and he had long purple hair and a Yugo, how would he act?

* * *

It's so often the dogma, and its inherent inference of guilt, that keeps people from even considering embracing a life of Christian faith. The vision of a bearded guy with scraggly hair wearing an off-white robe tied at the waist with a rope, wearing dust-covered sandals, teaching his followers from the banks of the Jordan River—that and all the rest of the best-known images and stories from the Bible unfortunately turn many people off.

As far as a personal conversation with a God they cannot see, many remain unconvinced of the power of prayer.

* * *

Frank does not in any way believe that God is a request center. For example, he cannot pray for a new Mercedes to—*poof!*—arrive in the driveway next week, as that's unrealistic and not how God works. Yet he believes that God gives us the knowledge and tools we need to achieve godly dreams and aspirations. God gives many gifts, recognized and appreciated or not.

When young Frank arrived in Florida as a naïve 18-year-old from Indiana, he felt very alone. He had no friends, no contacts, no network, no money, and no degree. He had barely graduated from high school with a 1.8 GPA. He spent many evenings in his tiny room in the cheap, one-bedroom apartment he'd rented with two other maintenance workers. Lying on his bed (a blow-up pool raft covered with a sheet), he would stare at the ceiling and ponder the big questions. *Where am I headed in this new place? What will become of my life?*

Young Frank arriving in Florida

It was during this lonely and scary time that he got back in touch with the faith of his youth, a faith that had sustained him in the past.

* * *

The story of the prodigal son is one of the best-known parables in the Bible, one that Frank knows maybe too well. A father has two boys, the older one an upstanding young man who does everything asked of him and the younger one who is wayward. The younger son asks his father for his inheritance then recklessly squanders it all on such worldly pleasures as wine and women. Eventually, money and hope gone, he returns home, repentant, believing he is no longer worthy of being called his father's son. But his delighted father welcomes him back with open arms, rejoicing and calling for a feast to celebrate (though the dutiful older brother is not pleased). This father's welcome is a metaphor for the promise of God's love and the Kingdom of Heaven: Grace, mercy, forgiveness, and redemption abound when one asks sincerely and with repentance.

The prodigal son goes off the rails just once, and after this one transgression, all is well. Unfortunately, Frank has become the "prodigal son" many, many times over. He has repeatedly squandered the gifts he has been given, and now, his current health condition reminds him very much of that time in his life when he would be flat on his back, trying to get comfortable on his cheap raft bed and feeling very alone as he wondered into the wee hours of the morning what the next bleak day would bring. Back then, Frank had gone through acceptance, denial, and disidentification, though he would not have been able to name them at the time. Most important, he had managed to tap back into his faith, too.

Grace, mercy, forgiveness, and redemption abound when one asks sincerely and with repentance.

This had occurred more than once, more than a few times, and it happened in a very big way starting on March 11, 2020, the day Frank received his possible death sentence. The prodigal son returns. Again.

* * *

Over the years, many people have asked Frank, "Have you always had faith?"

His answer: "Yes, but sometimes I have forgotten how to practice it." It is not always easy to give credit where credit is due, meaning those times when you're on top of the world, money flowing in, career great, relationships happy. Many people, even those who call themselves believers, are tempted to credit their successes to their own efforts and hard work.

Over the years, many people have asked Frank, "Have you always had faith?" His answer: "Yes, but sometimes I have forgotten how to practice it."

Sometimes, Frank certainly has done this, too. Like most fallible humans, he can forget. Eventually he always brings himself back to reality: These blessings are the good Lord at work, and all he has are gifts from Him (with lots of help from Nilsa, too). Frank has been in this battle with himself constantly throughout his life.

So, as Frank is rounding the corner to full recovery, he must keep in mind that all his progress is the result of fervent prayer and belief and many, many conversations with God. He has asked countless times for grace (to be free from this condition), mercy for anything he has done that possibly contributed to causing it, as well as love and forgiveness. He seeks redemption on a regular basis in his journal, his Bible readings, his daily Rosaries, and his heartfelt prayers.

NILSA'S STORY

Long before I even met Frank, I stepped into any encounter and everything I did with my faith. There is nothing that I do in my life without it. My faith is what keeps me upright every single day and gives me the strength to deal with whatever comes my way that I must handle.

So leaning into my faith at the time of Frank's illness was a very natural and automatic thing to do. At no point did I ever connect seriously with the possibility of the many poor outcomes that frequently seemed quite imminent. I always had faith that Frank's illness would work out the way it was meant to work out. In offering that faith up, I was able to do whatever it was God wanted me to do, both as Frank's wife and his unofficial nurse, to get him to the next day, and ultimately across that finish line.

At the very worst moments, when he was completely unable to do the things he loved so much and had always taken for granted—running, having endless energy, a full head of hair, public speaking, his writing, his real estate artistry, and so on—there was always a concern, healthwise, of what level he would ever be able to return to. Would he ever regain his vitality? We were in uncharted waters with this diagnosis, meaning we could only go by research and doctors' prognoses, which can certainly send anyone spiraling down a dark hole. Faith was Frank's ballast and kept him balanced throughout.

I have mentioned that Dr. Garcia was an angel on earth who was delivered directly to us just when we needed him most. I was so grateful for his knowledge, presence, and care, but surprised? No, because I can name numerous times God has delivered similar angels in human form to us during difficult challenges.

For the entire time I have known him, Frank has always been a relentless negotiator. He always wants better terms, a sweeter deal, more and better anything. Tell Frank flat out, "This is what I've got to offer, and that's it . . . ," and you'd better believe he will counter with something that gives him just what he needs. He always manages to get a little bit more out of any negotiation than what is offered at the outset and during what I am sure he considers only the first round.

Oddly, he practices that tactic and approach with God, too. He asks for everything he can think of, and then he and God negotiate. Frank's relationship with God is an incredibly special back-and-forth, fully engaged ongoing series of dialogues. Frank holds an actual conversation with Him every day. That is not unusual, but how those conversations have evolved during the various stages of our marriage has been so interesting.

Frank has never been afraid to challenge God. "I don't want to sound ungrateful, but this is not working. I need more. Soon. Now!" Over the years, he has begun to express in his daily conversations a new level of gratitude. And as the months of recovery passed, I saw a noticeable shift to an even more grateful and accepting attitude. Frank is now far more cautious and deliberate with all health matters. More careful in how he moves forward. He has become far more aware of what he can push his body to do. *What will be the end result if I do this today? How am I going to feel tomorrow and next week?* He now asks these kinds of questions. Different, but it is such a good and welcome change

While his prayers and thoughts are with God on a daily basis, Frank sometimes still challenges what God puts in front of him as his fate. He may challenge it for a long time, putting up quite a battle. However, he eventually always comes full circle, back to faith and acceptance of God's will. Sooner rather than later, 99 times out of 100 he recognizes that God's will is for Frank's betterment.

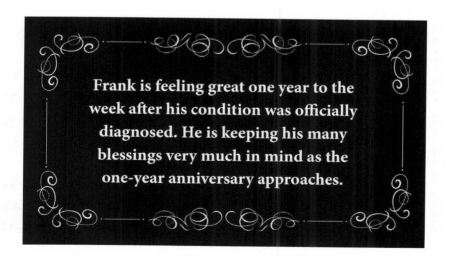

Frank is feeling great one year to the week after his condition was officially diagnosed. He is keeping his many blessings very much in mind as the one-year anniversary approaches.

FRANK'S JOURNAL

THREE CONSECUTIVE JOURNAL ENTRIES, 2021

(March 13)

I'm sitting in the Adirondack chair on our second-floor deck, and it's a beautiful sunny day. I remember one year ago today, after feeling sicker and sicker, I would sit right here with no energy, awaiting the confirmation of those first test results, wondering if I was going to die. I watched all the people across the street, jogging and walking along the path. How I wanted to join them! Now one year later, I have so much more energy than I did then.

I must be sure I don't do anything to jeopardize this progress with my body and my soul. Put my impulsive decisions through the constructive/destructive filter. By now I certainly know the difference. It could all be undone in the time it takes to make one unwise decision. I pray that God stays with me, helps me, and never leaves my side.

Man, I feel good! Stay high on life and my progress. It's amazing to think how good God has been to me and my family in every way. Be so grateful for that. Having my health back is plenty. I do not need to amplify it.

Right here, right now is all I need!

Thank you for the awareness you have given me, Lord. I'm doing my best to apply it in a way that makes you proud. Yes, I will have scares. It's what I do with those scares that will determine my progress in life. Keep me close to you and keep returning all my health, both physical and mental.

(March 15)

I am sitting on the wooden bench on the front porch after a six-mile run; I hadn't run in a week. Sadly, I feel my running days might be numbered, but I will keep going until I can't anymore.

When we visited Vinny yesterday by the lake, he said to Nilsa and me, "You guys are my best friends." This simple statement, from a formerly homeless man who rarely speaks more than just a few words, is the only one I need to hear this week.

"I've never had friends, in my entire life, like you guys." This is truly the voice of Jesus.

It's hard for me to look back and realize how close to dying I really was.

I want to thank you, Lord, for placing Vinny in our lives. I know I have done your will when it comes to caring for him. I just want to do things like that for the rest of my life. His words brought tears to my eyes, and they represent what is good in life. Keep me from all that obscures these shining moments.

It's hard for me to look back and realize how close to dying I really was. As I sit here, I am beyond grateful for all God has done for me. I don't want to ever forget this feeling, and the best way I can show my appreciation is to live in a way that always respects and appreciates the gift of life God has given me. Always respect how loving he has been to me; don't show disrespect by sinning. Remember, repeated sinful thoughts lead to feelings, and those feelings could lead to action.

Rise above and pray for strength. He has given me strength in the past and will do so again. I pray for a good week, Lord, and for good news.

Thank you for my awareness.

It is a significant day already when stunning news arrives. Frank has prayed so many times for his health to be restored. But answers to prayer come in God's time, not Frank's—another hard lesson he struggles with. Still, Frank can honestly say that every prayer he has ever asked for has been answered. Maybe not in the way he asked for it, and maybe the result is not what he envisioned, but absolutely, they have all been heard and acknowledged. This is a moment Frank has been praying for since that fateful March 11 day just over a year ago, a moment he never thought would come but believed it would. An epiphanous and extraordinarily golden moment of prayers answered!

FRANK'S JOURNAL

(March 17, 2021)

Today is my friend Mike Magi's birthday. When I prayed after communion at church I felt a special bond with him, not only remembering our friendship, but our similar diagnoses. His AML began with an A (acute ML) and mine (CML) began with a C (chronic ML). The rare case where it pays to have a C instead of an A! I joke, but I'm really having trouble today: missing my friend, knowing it so easily could have been me instead of him, or going right along with him to his new place in heaven.

But as I sit here thinking of him, I must include this: I got the good news I've been waiting to hear for more than a year! How many times did I write about getting my energy back and pray that my condition would go away completely? Well, I finally got what I've been waiting and praying for: quadruple zeroes in my PCR test. That's right, my BCR/ABL results read 0.000 percent—absolutely no trace of what nearly took my life one year ago.

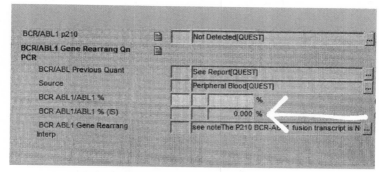

BCR/ABL1 p210		Not Detected[QUEST]
BCR/ABL1 Gene Rearrang Qn PCR		
BCR/ABL Previous Quant		See Report[QUEST]
Source		Peripheral Blood[QUEST]
BCR ABL1/ABL1 %		%
BCR ABL1/ABL1 % (IS)		0.000 %
BCR ABL1 Gene Rearrang Interp		see noteThe P210 BCR-ABL1 fusion transcript is N

A tearfully joyous day. The intruder is gone!

I am so grateful for this blessing. I want to do nothing to overshadow this joy. I want to praise you, Lord, with thanksgiving forever in my prayers.

You're *never* alone

Nilsa radiates peace and calm. To Frank she is a Mary-like presence, as she is the one to whom everyone turns: friends, family, their daughter, neighbors. She is a quiet and almost retiring figure at his many events, but for years many have noticed her special aura as well.

ILSA'S STORY

Many people go to church and memorize all the prayers there are to memorize. They can quote long passages from the Bible, know every hymn, preach theology inside out. But to me, personally, that is not what living your faith is about.

I genuinely believe that God puts things in front of me because he knows I am ready for them. Along the way, he puts me through tests to prepare for the real challenges . . . so I'll be ready. Sometimes, we are used as tools for others, as I was during Frank's health challenge. I always know I am being watched. My actions count, my reactions count, my words count. I must strive to make my actions God's mirror. That's just the way I live and have for decades.

This is the furthest thing from difficult for me. Other people find this a little hard to believe given some of the events I have come through. I have been tested to the moon and back! I believe that how we take that test and turn it into something good is what matters. Offering these challenges up to God is simple and easy. It is not easy to endure the pain of certain experiences, but I trust Him enough to believe he is always holding my hand throughout the process.

I must strive to make my actions God's mirror.

People have asked me how I seem so serene: "You're so soft-spoken and self-assured and unruffled." Or "You're so understanding and nonjudgmental." These descriptions all seem to end with some version of, "I want what you have."

And I ask, "What, exactly, do you see in me that you want?"

Peace. That's the word they use the most.

My response to this is to tell them the process must be natural.

My peace comes from knowing I am never alone. My faith and experience show me that I am guided at every step of the way. This is the only way I get through anything: knowing God is holding me. If I thought I was alone, my knees would buckle at every turn. I am never alone. In challenging times, His presence is even stronger. When I am struggling, I can feel his presence right next to me, his arm around me. That support keeps me on my feet and moving.

I think what people want when they ask me this is a secret-something they can quickly do to "get" the qualities they perceive in me, but all I can say is that my demeanor comes naturally from years and decades of practicing my faith—and most of all, my peace with the path I am on, whether or not it is one I planned. The acceptance of one's life and how it has unfolded, or how it continues to unfold, is where you find true peace.

Accept how your life is unfolding while using your best efforts to move forward. My life is by no means perfect. Far from it. But I try to step into each new day with my faith as my guide. Every forward step is because God has asked me to live in this fashion.

The acceptance of one's life and how it has unfolded, or how it continues to unfold, is where you find true peace.

This could be doing something as simple as texting a friend who is struggling. Almost daily, early in the morning when my heart is most open and alive, I will somehow sense that this friend or family member needs prayer, and nearly every time the text comes back: "How did you know?"

This form of love, with the prompting of the Holy Spirit, is something small and easy for me to do and simply flows out of me. Sometimes I read the texts later and do not even remember sending them out.

That's how I practice my faith, and it's how I try to share it as well.

This kind of peace is within everyone's reach. There is no perfection in faith; there's only practice. Lots and lots of practice.

For those readers who practice some form of faith (or who are simply curious), put your bookmarker on this page, close your book, and take another look at its ethereal front cover. The rope reaching up into the clouds and into the heavens represents the promise of faith. At the other end of the rope is Frank's hand (and your hand), bloodied from hanging on so tightly during adversity. That tiny, fraying thread between the heavens and the hand represents how close the difference between life and death can be, whether quite literally or in a more figurative sense.

Look closely where the top of that rope is going. See the soothing light shining down from above. Yes, that divine dimension is the promise of hope, the promise of faith that awaits if you *just* hang on and know that you are not alone. God will *never*, ever let you go.

> **That tiny, fraying thread between the heavens and the hand represents how close the difference between life and death can be, whether quite literally or in a more figurative sense.**

TRY THIS WHEN YOU'RE
(NOT) ALONE

- If you are a believer—someone who practices a religion or professes faith in some form of the divine—take a few minutes to *respectfully* and *without judgement* ponder how someone who is an atheist or agnostic might manage the adversity you are facing. If you did not believe in God nor had any faith, how would you approach your adversity? Please visit Adversitology.com or *Adversitology's* Instagram feed and share your "opposites" story. You'll see a place for "Believer's Non-Belief" stories. Or post your ideas on Facebook or Instagram and use the hashtag #Adversitology. Six months after the release of *Adversitology* one story from this category and the person who wrote that story will be randomly picked to share a weekend with Frank at his "glass cabin" in North Carolina.

- And if you don't follow any religion nor have any belief in a supreme being(s), you too switch places. *Respectfully* and *with an open mind,* if you were to accept for a moment that there is a God that you could believe in and faithfully count on in times of adversity, what would you do? How would you start a dialogue/prayer regarding the fear associated with your adversity? Just as above, visit Adversitology.com or *Adversitology's* Instagram feed and share your "opposites" story. You'll see a place for "Non-Believer's Belief" stories. Or post your ideas on Facebook or Instagram and use the hashtag #Adversitology. Six months after the release of *Adversitology* one story from this category and the person who wrote it will be randomly picked to share a weekend with Frank at his "glass cabin" in North Carolina.

8 | TIME TO TERMINATE

Clash Not with Reality, But Create Your Own

Winston Churchill once said, "Now, this is not the end. It is not even the beginning of the end. But it is, perhaps, the end of the beginning."

There is enormous relief and happiness, joy and celebration for Frank and his family when that amazing quadruple-zero reading arrives for the first time. It's 1:11 p.m. on March 17, 2021, just six days after the one-year anniversary of his diagnosis, and Dr. Garcia has texted a screenshot to Frank's phone. This prompts plenty of sincere gratitude and a new resolve on Frank's part, as he knows that a single 0.000 percent reading is not nearly "the end."

Nope, adversities just don't end that way.

Another full year of diligence will pass before March of 2022, when Frank is able to determine that it's time to "terminate" and that his adversity is officially over. For good.

During that time, the full life that Frank enjoyed for decades slowly returns. His ability to expand his bandwidth is also expanding. The Renaissance man is back! Frank plots a return to Badwater. He and Nilsa decide to put their home of 25 years on the market and relocate. He decides to "unretire" from creating real estate artistry and kicks off the process by scripting and starring in two short films to tease the comeback, which hints at, then depicts, a completely new, mind-blowing, colonizing-the-moon location. Ideas for his eighth book (the one you're holding in your hands now) are forming.

Frank has worked so hard during the two years he had his condition that it eventually leads to the creation and implementation of this A-D-V-E-R-S-I-T-Y plan. A simple, hopeful, and disciplined initiative that taught Frank, and now you, how to overcome adversity when we're barely hanging on by a thread.

Looking back since that first 0.000 percent text in March of 2021, Frank can see his growth in mastering disidentification and savoring everything while clinging to nothing. Now, he refuses to attach too much weight to either his condition or the latest great news. He continues to talk with Nilsa and Dr. Garcia and to pour out his heart in his journals, but it's without nearly as much of that overwhelming feeling of fitful, dread-filled nervous energy dragging him down.

Frank also realizes that he may have self-inflicted some unnecessary anxiety and pain over the year between his first 0.000 percent reading and now. He feels he could have said, and believed, "This is it, all you wanted. You got your freaking quadruple-zero reading, and now you're done," much sooner. Just a year ago, he couldn't quite manage to do that—although it would have been justified.

His growth and progress have continued organically and slowly. Over the past year Frank toggled back and forth a bit with some days when he was weak, or tired, or just generally didn't feel that great. Why? Was it the inevitable process of aging? Or was it a haunting reminder from the ghost of the intruder, which he thinks of as "Cease. Move. Leave." in place of its medical name or initials?

Instead of every day, Frank has been writing in his journal every other day, or every few days. Yes, the act was once part of his almost-daily routine, and there is a written entry about some aspect of his health adversity nearly every day for two solid years. But after the initial fantastic news, his habit of daily journaling has slowly tapered down.

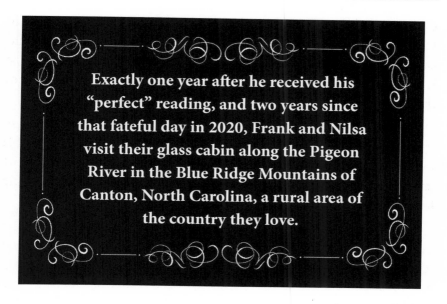

Exactly one year after he received his "perfect" reading, and two years since that fateful day in 2020, Frank and Nilsa visit their glass cabin along the Pigeon River in the Blue Ridge Mountains of Canton, North Carolina, a rural area of the country they love.

FRANK'S JOURNAL

(March 2022)

We are in North Carolina on this cold Saturday morning. In a chair facing the snow-dusted mountains, I sit here a completely cured man. There has been no trace of the intruder in my body for over a year. That's right, I've had a reading of 0.000 percent since March 9, 2021—for 12 consecutive months! I have been waiting to write these words for two freaking years:

Completely CURED!!

At my last visit with Dr. Garcia, he said I could stop taking Sprycel, the medicine that has passed my lips and into my mouth every day for the past two years. I have now attained the holy grail of recovery: treatment-free remission from an illness that could have taken my life. I can stop the medication altogether! But rather than do that, I choose to take a small trace for a brief time just to be safe. After all, Dr. Garcia initially wanted me on the medication for three full years.

I just looked back through my running history. I see that it was exactly two years ago, in March of 2020, I went wobbling out of our driveway and crossed A1A to the low wall on the other side. I barely made it. Today, I will go out and run a 10K through the mountains of Canton, NC. Sure, I'll be a bit slow, but I'll be running as a healthy man.

That's enough, Frank. You have received the most important gift for which you have ever prayed. In two years, you have received 100 percent of your health back. One more time:

Completely CURED!!

Frank doesn't write in his journal again for a month, and his resolve to continue taking even a tiny bit of medicine lasts for only two weeks. Even that minuscule maintenance dose serves as an unwanted daily reminder of the past issue, and he's over it. Because on that spring day in 2022, helpfully noted in his journal, he chose to terminate his journey through this health adversity. He can actually track the exact date he calls "time's up" on this adversity, a milestone that's usually quite difficult to pinpoint.

While musing about "time's up," he remembers something that happened a few weeks earlier.

One day as he and Nilsa relaxed on the couch in the family room, Frank glanced over and really paid attention to a tiny wicker chair that Laura used to sit in by the fireplace. He said, "Honey, do you realize there was a day, many years ago, when our little girl sat in that chair for the last time? We have no idea when that day was, or even what year. We didn't know she would rock back and forth in it for the last time. Even she didn't know it was the last time!"

Laura still small enough to sit in her wicker chair

Laura's attachment to this chair had terminated, quite naturally, because the time came when she grew too big to comfortably fit in it. She moved on without a backward glance, as did her parents, and no one could even remember when the final day had come.

*L*AURA'S STORY

There comes a point when I am feeling down when I recite one of my favorite sayings: "I'm sick and tired of being sick and tired." That's my go-to phrase to motivate myself when I'm in a rut or need to be proactive about ending a cycle that I know is not good for me. When I'm sick and tired I feel drained; I just want to hide and mope. So I always remind myself that life goes in cycles, and sometimes, it's time to stomp it out and terminate a bad cycle.

It's easy for young people like me to get bogged down. We're getting so much information from the world that tells us who we need to be, what we need to strive for, what date we need to accomplish it by. This can create overwhelming pressure when we're trying to figure out the big questions:

Should I marry this person? Do I want children soon or ever? What is my profession going to be? Who and what do I want to become at work?

I have felt these pressures. I feel as if every year that ticks by in my twenties brings more expectations. Sometimes I just don't know what to do, who to ask, or which way is up. It feels easier just to give up and pull the covers over my head, to take the easy way out. One that doesn't necessarily fulfill my highest potential.

I'm experiencing many major life checkpoints these days, and the best thing about them is that I no longer brood over what used to really bother me only a year ago. This is growth, which is probably exponential at this time, and it feels great. I had challenges in college, for sure, but the process moved itself along quite efficiently. I would take the correct courses for my major, pass them, and then graduate. There was a natural, orderly progression. I couldn't get stuck there, and the endpoint was always in sight.

Now, ongoing daily life is more of a beautiful mystery.

Going out into the real world is so different. Now it's my responsibility to move things along for myself. I'm no longer following anyone else's timetable or schedule. It's time to be proactive in my own life, a feeling that can be somewhat new to many recent graduates. In college, final exams or worrying about my grades could put me in a bad headspace. But I always knew that if I could just push through, spring break was next, then summer—and no classes! Now, ongoing daily life is more of a beautiful mystery.

It's a life where I now accept that mystery while creating my own path. Jobs, apartments, bills. There's no longer a feeling of "Get through that, then I can breathe." Challenges are constant and without interruption. I have come to realize that one of the most important tasks in adult life is making sure I consciously terminate cycles that are no longer good for me rather than allow them to terminate on their own.

If you were to look back at all the adversities you've gone through in your life, you know there came a day when you "got over it." Maybe it was simply that enough time passed, or you moved on to something or someone new, recovered from the accident or illness, had a financial windfall. Whatever the case, all adversities eventually pass (reread the Blue-Sky section from Chapter 2). On some ordinary unnoticed day, you will cease thinking or worrying about something that once completely consumed you. That's because it's really, truly, over.

Suffering doesn't go on into eternity. If it did, we would all die trying to manage our first serious adversity.

Yes, it's over, that which once seemed so incomprehensible, impossible, and insurmountable to overcome is now gone! Can you remember the exact day you stopped thinking about your ex, for example, the one who broke your heart, the one that got away? The answer is no, of course; it's now a hazy memory, in the past, one you might even recall with *fond* nostalgia. The only good thing about your breakup from your boyfriend or girlfriend, divorce, bankruptcy, estrangement from a loved one, firing, health scare, death of a friend, and so on is that they *do* terminate.

Suffering doesn't go on into eternity. If it did, we would all die trying to manage our first serious adversity. We would suffer a heart attack or stress ourselves into a breakdown because we never, ever believe that this pain will end or that we can indeed cope. But we *did* get through it, and we will continue to do so with every single adversity in our lives.

* * *

While running his businesses Frank has been involved in a few unpleasant legal controversies. (To be fair, there's no such thing as a pleasant one.) People have sued him and done their best to shut him and his companies down for good. There have been horrible, trying times over the years when he's faced foreclosure on a multimillion-dollar oceanfront spec home that would lead to complete financial ruin. And when he and Nilsa came close to splitting up, those were his darkest relationship adversities imaginable. They were tremendously stressful times, but Frank doesn't even think about these events anymore. They're in the rearview mirror and instead, as always, he chooses to fix his gaze on what he can see through his crystal-clear windshield.

The mental and emotional torture brought about by these events has been purged. The demon has been exorcised and is now completely gone for good.

> **Frank doesn't even think about these events anymore. They're in the rearview mirror and instead, as always, he chooses to fix his gaze on what he can see through his crystal-clear windshield.**

*   *   *

So, the big question is this: Can you get there? To adversity terminated, purged, over, in your rearview mirror? Can you do it a little bit faster, with less pain and agony along the way?

Yes! The $25 or so that you have invested in this book will pay off. Do what you've learned here, and you are empowered to *terminate* your adversity quicker and with less pain. That's easier said than done, for sure, like several of the steps in this process. But at this point, it's time. You're ready. This comes from performing every step so far along the way of A-D-V-E-R-S-I. This awareness would not be present had you not done all the hard work to arrive here, in the middle of T!

Adversity doesn't come when it's convenient for you. It might not wait until you have recovered from a current difficulty before some unwelcome guest arrives on your doorstep. We all know how one adversity can lead to another and how truly daunting it is to have to face more than one at a time. However, now you have a blueprint for the next time. Let *this* one be behind you.

Create your own termination date instead of just allowing it to fade (hopefully) from memory. Don't wait for some day far in the future to look back and say, "Wow, I never really even think about that adversity anymore." Right now—yes, this very minute—call time to terminate. Be proactive. *You* have the capability to create that moment in time!

You are qualified, deserving, worthy, and ready for your *time to terminate*. You *do* have control over when and where that finish line is drawn. And that old saying, "time heals all wounds"? Well, that time is now. Realize just how many things in your life are truly within your control.

(And if you're saying to yourself that you're still not ready or not worthy, that's untrue but understandable. You do have one more chapter to go: "Y Not You?")

* * *

The mind wills the body to do what the mind wants—and do what the body does not want. Frank knows this to be true due to his devotion to ultramarathons. When you show up for Badwater, the toughest footrace of them all, you must be ready, both mentally and physically. In three out of his five DNFs at Badwater (Did Not Finish), it was his mind that failed him. Only two DNF races were due to a physical ailment (serious heart issues in 2012 and a torn tendon in his foot in 2019). Oh, there were good reasons to quit in his other three DNFs—feet covered in blisters, distorted state of mind, dehydration, fainting facedown on the pavement from exhaustion— but those DNFs, at their core, were truly failures of Frank's mind. Frank's mindset was not where it needed to be, the place it was on the seven times he triumphantly crossed the Badwater ultramarathon finish line.

Creating your own *time to terminate* is one of the most empowering things you will ever do.

Struggling but not defeated, at the edge of a Badwater DNF

$\mathcal{L}$AURA'S STORY

Before I graduated and left for New York, I was a high achiever in college. I was so involved with my university as student body president, well-known on campus, and I managed to graduate with a 3.0 despite a really rough final semester. It all went so fast, and even though I always felt I was well prepared and ready to leave college, when it ended so abruptly, I wasn't quite there. Many of my peers want to hang on to the college experience for years and years, but for me, I always saw it as a four-year stop along the way to something bigger.

Leaving that bubble, where so many things came so easily to me, and being thrust into the locked down job market of 2020 really threw me into a dark place. I lost so much momentum after going 100 miles per hour for years. Suddenly I was not even at zero. I was confined to my parents' house, no graduation ceremony, no job prospects, and my dad was so sick. Yes, things were going backwards, and it was not an enjoyable time.

My brain was spinning; everything had been suddenly thrust into reverse. I felt so stuck and frustrated. It was really tough. It's hard to tell someone in a depressive mindset to just get going, take action, but that's what it came down to for me. *If it's meant to be, it will happen. You'll get over it. Other people have it worse.* Those platitudes people try to comfort you with don't help. For me, it was simple. When I hit the wall, I reminded myself: *Just have fun.* Those three words have gotten me out of small and big funks, reminding me that I'm missing out on so many moments that could be great if I weren't cooped up in my bed ruminating.

I read a terrific book, a bestseller called *Play: How It Shapes the Brain, Opens the Imagination, and Invigorates the Soul* by Stuart Brown and Christopher Vaughan, and I found it so inspiring. Fun is the best part of the human experience! I would read and reflect on many of the fantastic times and wonderful things I had enjoyed in the past. I can easily recall the top five days of my life and how I felt on each of them. I realized that I wanted to feel those emotions once again, and it wouldn't happen by myself in my room. I knew I could experience more "best days" again once I got moving and out the door.

At the height of the pandemic, I moved to the heart of locked down New York City, where the job market was dead, to put it bluntly.

In business and my personal life, other good days are ahead. I can close my eyes, picture those moments, and remind myself I want more.

In November of 2020 I decided enough was enough. I thought things would improve, and I thought this cycle would end on its own, but it didn't. It was time to violate fate, to do something radical. It had been a long eight months, and Dad had just completed his Yugo We-go Tour—he was clearly so much better. So, at the height of the pandemic, I moved to the heart of locked down New York City, where the job market was dead, to put it bluntly.

This excited me; I knew this major change would shock me for good or bad. I would certainly be starting over!

I'm like my dad in temperament: we feel our highs to the extreme, and we take our lows badly. Sometimes it's hard to keep on an even keel. The lows are paralyzing, and the adversity seems too much. That period of adversity ended the day I arrived in NYC. I flew in a day early to get my keys from the property owner and my parents met me the next day with all my stuff from Florida in a U-Haul. Here was the upside to all the many downsides of moving at that time: I got a great apartment, for a great deal, in a fantastic neighborhood. I got to relax and get to know the city when it was quiet.

Laura: Queen of NYC!

It was not a seamless transition, as I have mentioned before, but I had wanted this life since I was a little girl. I am so glad I took the chance. I wake up every day and feel incredibly lucky to be in the exact place I had envisioned since I was a kid. And now it's not a dream! I am right here!

I will always remember this decision to terminate the adversity I had been experiencing for eight months and begin a whole new life, because it was such a momentous change. There will be plenty more up and down cycles ahead, but for now, I am a busy, happy New Yorker looking forward to celebrating my first quarter-century on the planet soon! Am I glad I implemented "Time to Terminate"? Oh, hell yes!

FRANK'S JOURNAL

(April 2022, one month since my last entry)

Today I go to see Dr. Garcia. Every six weeks I'm reminded of what was and no longer is. I want you to know, Lord, that I will never stop being grateful for the cure you blessed me with. I choose to no longer write about it because there's no reason to give it any more thought. I don't want to take the chance to awaken the beast. You healed me. My faith in you healed me.

There will come a time when I will be able to share this blessing, full on, with the world. I'm not quite ready yet. Or, better put: my ego and sense of infallibility aren't ready. We are all flawed; I hope to free myself from this type of ego and let this story be told . . .

The seed is planted. Frank knows the time is near when he is going to write about and tell the world what he has kept to himself and shared with only five other people. Not long after the seed is planted it begins to germinate.

One day, as Frank and Nilsa are lying in bed after sleeping in, he suddenly says to her, "I think it's time."

He has been talking with a man who has a blood disorder, and Frank is urging him to accept what has happened, not to give it any of his energy, violate fate, and so on. It occurs to Frank that he is helping one person to improve his mindset going forward, and maybe he could help many others by vulnerably sharing the story of his illness and how he overcame the adversity it represented.

TERMINATE NOW

Assuming you're reading this while in the middle of some adversity, or even experiencing one or more that may be just lingering around, it's time to create your own reality.

It's time for you to declare your current adversity terminated *right now*. If you're still not sure, go ahead and read the final "Y Not You" chapter and the epic epilogue, but come back to this page and fill in the blank below. Why not use a red pen? It will remind you of all the blood, sweat, and tears you endured to get to this point to be able to declare your adversity terminated for good.

Today, my time to terminate has come.

On this date, _____,

I, _____,

have terminated the adversity I refer to as

_____

_____.

Now, take it a step further. Let other readers help you stay accountable. Go to Adversitology.com and share with the world your brave choice to terminate. Go there and read stories from others to help you know that you are not alone in your desire to terminate your current adversity.

P.S. Remember Laura's reference to the "top 5 days of her life?" You'll find them on Adversitology.com!

9 Y NOT YOU?

Why *not* you?

James Allen counseled, "For true success ask yourself these four questions: Why? Why not? Why not me? Why not now?"

Congratulations! You have now earned your Ph.D. in Adversitology. You're no longer barely hanging on by a thread just trying to survive.

You've invested your open-minded energy and implemented the action items at the end of each chapter. All that enlightened and precious energy you expended will now be returned to you for the rest of your life, anytime you wish to call upon it. It's now yours for the taking, and there should be no doubting your hard-won new wisdom. You absolutely have both the ability and the necessary new tools to not only leave your current adversity behind you, but you can also be far better equipped to deal with whatever curveballs life will throw at you in the future. Not to mention, you are likely now in an empowered, informed new state of mind, enabling you to help others who are going through their own challenges.

Whether you picked up this book for help with combating a specific situation or simply want to be prepared and enlightened for the future, you have come a long way on your journey.

Let's review.

1. You know to *accept* the reality that yes, this adversity did indeed happen to you. You consider the adversitology quotient: the idea that every person on this earth faces an equal amount of adversity, and yours is no more severe or debilitating than anyone else's. Sure, there is plenty of denial at first, the mind's way of protecting you from shockingly unwelcome news. But you realize this is a defense mechanism that will—and does— end soon, and it's time to be proactive.

Remember: Sitting still and refusing to accept your adversity will not make it go away, and it *will* prolong the agony.

So you rate your personal situation on the Adversitometer and search your soul while considering to what degree this misfortune was an external bolt from the blue or possibly a result of some of your own actions. Yes, you understand that every adversity falls into *only* two categories: external (innocent) or self-inflicted (consequential). With an honest self-assessment, you place yours in the appropriate one. You do your research on your particular condition, but you don't get lost in a black hole of too much information and conflicting opinions. And then you get moving, leaving denial, blame, anger, resentment, and "Why me?" behind. Time to act and face your adversity down!

2. You have learned to *disidentify*, to give your adversity no energy. You realize that you can become tightly tied to your adversity through the energy you expend to fight it. By fighting your adversity, you empower it, so instead you refuse to allow this temporary roadblock to take over your entire life and your every waking moment.

Remember the dictionary definition: disidentification is simply "a benign separation from one's sense of self, a stepping-stone away from self-identity to attempt to observe oneself objectively." You ponder the "I vs. me" conundrum (hint: "I" is the soul) and the Blue Sky theory, which says that all adversity is by nature is fleeting, over the grand scheme of a lifetime.

No absorption of adversity!

You accept that some good could come from the most devastating adversities and believe that lessening another's pain helps lessen your own. You keep in mind that by over-identifying with your demon, you give it power. You have done the hard work to understand the nature of your adversity, and the reason (if there is one) you allowed this into your life. You don't chase darkness out of the room with a knife or a broom and instead you turn on the light. It is through understanding that adversity slowly disappears. Frank's formula: No absorption of adversity!

What's yours?

3. You choose to *violate* fate in your own way, by filtering whatever others, however well-meaning, project onto your situation about how you should behave in the face of your adversity. You are the captain of your fate! This is the time to reject conventional or accepted wisdom if it doesn't resonate with you. You strive to make informed decisions after considering others' input, are not afraid to raise challenges, even with experts, and always give yourself the final call.

This is not to say you do not lean on trusted friends and family. Their support can be enormous. However, you refuse to collaborate with anyone with whom you do not personally connect and believe supports your growth throughout this journey. And you keep the circle of trusted collaborators small and tight, because you are the one in charge.

Challenge then change the mind of fate itself. You and only you will make the final determination of your fate, especially when faced with physical, financial, or relational adversity. Remember: Your fate comes from within, not without.

4. The hardest part for many: You commit to *Every. Single. Day.* Still, backsliding is part of the process, and you don't beat yourself up for briefly slipping into old habits. Of course you fall, more than once, but you quickly regroup by applying relentless forward motion. You overcome what seems an insurmountable obstacle, in large part by committing to "every single day" and reaping the imperceptible progress a string of such days, weeks, and months eventually brings.

You acknowledge that all progress is solely up to you. It is a simple but critical step to overcoming adversity: Get out there and start plugging away. Take action! (Get off your knees and start walking.) You do not fall prey either to distractibility or boredom in this quest. Sticking to new habits and routines is hard but oh-so-rewarding when you look back and see the progress you've made so far.

5. At the halfway point, it's time to take a moonshot: to *risk it* in a way that will shock you back to life. Time to remember the places and activities that you loved in your pre-adversity life and revisit or recreate such an experience now, as a simple reminder that you can and will enjoy them again someday soon. Time to take a break from the slow, methodical progress of every single day and shake things up. There's no need for a new normal, only a more frequent extraordinary.

You vow to invest all you can afford into this personal solo journey: time, money, and effort. That is not to say this emotional reset must be costly. The idea is to surround yourself with healing energy, preferably in nature, to promote enlightenment. You are all you have: You are the only person you will spend a lifetime with, so treasure your own company. You have carefully planned your own personal "risk-it adventure," and your departure is imminent.

6. While accomplishing all the above, you make sure not to get too attached to your progress, so you *savor everything and cling to nothing*. This starts with a searching examination of your own unhealthy attachments, which generally arise from a place of neediness. The desire to hold on too tightly and become dependent on those things that bring you pleasure can lead straight to addiction and unending misery.

High points and peak moments are wonderful. Clinging and desperately trying to hold onto them—not so great. Contrary to what your culture and religion may have taught you, nothing, absolutely nothing outside of you, can "make" you happy or bring you lasting joy. True happiness can only come from within. It does not come from attaining wealth or material goals or engaging in thrill-seeking behavior. You consider that the path to enlightenment is to surrender clinging and desire. No need to abandon regular life and take to a mountaintop to chant *Om* for the rest of your days, but getting off that hamster wheel of constantly doing, accomplishing, and attaining is a worthy personal goal.

7. Whether or not religious practice is a part of your life, you have the sense of *I am not alone.* You have considered what a profound difference faith (in anything!) can make when facing down serious adversity. To genuinely believe that you are not alone on this daunting journey is an immense source of comfort.

To whom do you pray? Your relationship and talks with God can take any form you want, and they begin with a simple conversation.

Nilsa shared her belief that a key component to enjoying a peaceful life is always accepting the path you are on, whether or not it is a direction or detour you planned for. It is much easier to move ahead every day with faith as your guide, particularly when times are tough.

If you are a non-believer, you give careful thought to how a believer might approach adversity, and if you do have a religion or a belief system with faith in a supreme being(s), you consider how someone who doesn't might manage adversity. (And remember, from those who share their stories on Adversitology.com, two winners will be chosen at random to spend a weekend with Frank at his Mountain Modern glass cabin along the Pigeon River in Canton, North Carolina!)

8. And finally, it's *time to terminate* the process laid out in this book. Believe it or not, it can be hard to let go of your own attachment to your adversity. *Time's up* means just that: You guard against lingering in this state of repair for any longer than you must. There is a natural end to suffering through adversity, as there is to almost any process in life. But you will take the initiative to choose your own termination date.

Laura revealed how she got sick and tired of being sick and tired about the stalled state of her life after college graduation. She chose a date and moved to New York City during the height of lockdown, where she began a new phase when she could thrive and be happy! Yes, time will eventually heal all wounds, but why wait if you don't have to? Don't keep your eyes on the rearview mirror. Instead, focus your gaze straight ahead, through the windshield from the driver's seat. Proactively terminating your adversity is one of the most empowering things you will ever do.

If you didn't do it in the last chapter (or would like to do it again), fill in the statement below:

Today, my time to terminate has come.

On this date, _____,

I, _____,

have terminated the adversity I refer to as

_____

_____ .

Still not convinced? Not 100 percent sure that you are brave enough, worthy enough, or have done enough work to move ahead and never look back? Read on . . .

✳ ✳ ✳

Hopefully, while reading each individual section in this book and going through the entire A-D-V-E-R-S-I-T-Y idea step by step, you've felt an exciting sense of aspiration, and you want to take (or already have taken) these initiatives and apply them to your own challenges. In the previous chapter you terminated the process. You were also advised to read this chapter if you weren't ready to terminate. Even if you are someone who named your adversity, then signed and dated that page and this page in red ink, what might happen in the not-too-distant future is predictable.

Any nagging doubts should have been silenced forever the minute you filled in those blanks, but suddenly doubts push their way back in. That negative little voice in your head can say, "My adversity is way worse than anyone realizes!" "This particular plan doesn't apply to my complicated situation." Or even, "I just don't think this is gonna work for me."

Nicely tell that voice in your head to be silent. Be selective in that silence and choose liberation. After a few attempts, if that voice still isn't

Be selective in that silence and choose liberation.

obeying you, then boldly and in front of the mirror tell it that you are in control and now it's time for it to shut up.

You have made it all the way to the Y chapter, so this book is most certainly for you. You would have tossed it aside a long time ago if some of these ideas weren't resonating. But you're here! You have absorbed many innovative ideas and hopefully implemented some new philosophies. Stand back from your problem and listen to that other voice in your head, the voice of reason: "Other people have applied these ideas and they work very well." So why not you? Again: Y (Why) Not You?!

Go ahead, apply these principles to your current or future adversity, or share this book with someone who is going through something, and watch this book work its magic. The finish line is in sight. It's not about the process; it's about the purpose! You can read a new self-help book every week and never change a thing. Why are you doing all this, following the A-D-V-E-R-S-I-T-Y letters? It's simple: to put this adversity behind you much quicker than it would otherwise take and do so with far less pain.

Why is it so hard for some people, maybe even you? What is causing that naysaying voice in their heads—their subconscious minds—to convince them that they can't do this, or it's not time, or this isn't for them? For those whose subconscious is *not* trying to talk them out of this, great! But for that other smaller yet significant percentage of people, let's talk for a moment about the power of the subconscious mind.

For starters, we human beings tend to feel very enthusiastic at the beginning of any sort of self-improvement journey (working out, quitting smoking, eating healthier, losing weight, going to church, and on and on). But we can run out of gas. We might lose sight of our aspirations along with the motivation to keep going, and that can lead to falling back into the same old patterns. That is often due to sheer boredom and inertia; the key is to *execute* your plans. (More on that in a moment.)

In this modern, screen-focused world, we have become more and more conditioned to negativity. Negative news gets more clicks. Rude comments get a reaction. At every turn, so much that we hear, see, post, read, and respond to can be somewhat negative. The subconscious mind has become conditioned to look for a reason to say no instead of yes. Another result of the social media revolution is that we all try hard to portray our best, most attractive selves, making sure we look and appear to be doing better than we really are in our lives. This tendency is simply a reality of modern life. So, when adversity strikes, we often try hard to portray the opposite, or ignore it entirely.

Put this adversity behind you much quicker than it would otherwise take, and do so with far less pain.

In terms of this book, these realities mean that some people will stumble just when they need to execute.

Know that a super-strong, almost otherworldly, desire to achieve something high and great can literally alter your DNA, just as it's described in the 364 pages of the book *Aspire!* Realize that you can indeed create your own reality and alter your DNA. You *can* kill the person you were born to be to become the person you want to be. We can change our very DNA at any moment in time, simply by choosing something new to aspire to. This requires a special twist on the principle of "every single day."

POINTERS FROM *ASPIRE!*

Imagine a clock to describe the stages people go through while attempting to attain their aspirations. It is simply a visual tool to give you a sense of the various checkpoints along the way. Straight-up 12 o'clock is "Running on Excitement." You're pumped, you're motivated, you can't wait to dive into this new way of life!

Three o'clock is "Don't Be a Flea," which means that when the initial burst of enthusiasm starts to fade you begin to think of excuses to quit, to jump off and flee. At this point we often hop around like fleas without stopping and working long enough to see results. Another hazard of modern life: It's hard to concentrate when there's always something new just one click away.

Six o'clock is "No Half-Assers Allowed." This represents the drudgery of putting in the work. Every. Single. Day. At six o'clock you're halfway there. It's where the rubber meets the road, and many people give up. It's just too hard. They don't like this new program. It isn't doing anything anyway. Instead, we should be looking at all the progress made so far and doubling down on perseverance.

Nine o'clock is almost one full revolution around the clock face, and you're on the upswing! This stage is "You Tied Your Own Shoes Together?" This is where a small number of people inexplicably find themselves stuck, unable to complete that final mile. This occurs when you associate too much with the process and forget about the true purpose.

Back at 12 o'clock again, the cycle is complete. You've done it, you've executed, your mission is complete. In the case of *Adversitology*, you have *terminated* your adversity. Reaching this stage will ideally bring about a feeling of immense pride and accomplishment that will carry over to other areas of life, even to future adversities that you will now overcome with boldness and confidence.

Execution is the daily application of aspiration. It's essential for turning vision and aspiration into results-driven reality.

When it comes time to alter your DNA—not only aspire to change but implement and execute—we sometimes don't feel worthy or ready. Recognize that this is merely your subconscious doing its best to find a way to allow you to quit. The subconscious can be quite a trickster, and when we listen to that false voice it frequently causes us to give up on our goals.

Stuff it down, clobber those voices as if you're playing Whac-A-Mole. It is only your subconscious speaking, and you are in control of your thoughts and your destiny. Approximately 2,350 new books will come out the day after you read this one, and you might be tempted to pick up one of those to get over your adversity. But why? You already hold in your hands a proven prescription, and you have a clearly spelled out process, so stick to your purpose.

Read *Adversitology* again if you feel it will benefit you. Read it as many times as you believe will help you get to the results you seek.

You already hold in your hands a proven prescription, and you have a clearly spelled out process, so stick to your purpose.

For a moment, think of the movie *The Wizard of Oz*. Remember the end, when the great and all-powerful Oz is unmasked as this frightened little man? One who is pushing buttons and pulling levers to create a false appearance of grandiosity, omnipotence, and self-importance?

When we're facing adversity and we pull back the curtain, every single one of us feels small and scared. There are no wizards to call on when we're struggling. We all must learn to help each other, and it is in this spirit of help and encouragement that this book came to be.

Because the other lesson from *The Wizard of Oz* is that the lion wasn't really cowardly; he bravely acted when his friends were in danger. The tin man had a heart, and the scarecrow had a brain. All three were used to help Dorothy on the perilous journey to Oz. The traits they wanted so badly were there all along, just as the ability to overcome adversity is inside you.

* * *

Frank is no wizard, but he does have the "magic" of A-D-V-E-R-S-I-T-Y to share, and the best way to see if it will work for you is to put it to the test.

Give it a try. You have nothing to lose, and every adversity put behind you to gain.

ILSA'S STORY

Almost 40 years ago, I was away at college when my mom was diagnosed with cancer. I immediately left school to go home and care for her. I was 20 years old; it was just me, my mom, and my dad. The outlook was grim. Her doctors told me, "Your mother has at most six months to live."

Times were quite different then. For one thing, there were limited options on how to treat cancer. The choices were few and all the treatments brutal on the patient's body and mind. There was no Internet for research or just to find others in a similar circumstance for support and advice.

How I would have loved a guide on that lonely, rocky path!

My mother was desperately ill, shrinking down to 90 pounds as the months passed. I was so hungry for any resources that might help us. No, I was desperate for the slightest scrap of information I could find about her condition and how to be a more effective caregiver as my world grew smaller and smaller. It would have meant the world to me then to hear from somebody who'd come out the other side as my mother eventually did, but not before we completed an arduous, eight-year journey to full remission. I am so grateful that my mother is still with us today.

As life went on and the years passed, I would never again be caught off guard when it came to unexpected challenges in life. When Frank's situation arose, not once did I allow myself to entertain the possibility of him not prevailing. I knew that his return to full health was possible, even probable, and that seed of hope-turned-belief was enough to keep me going every day. I would support my husband all the way to the finish line. We were going to get there together. I saw no other outcome.

One of my favorite passages from the Bible is from the Gospel of Matthew, 17:20: "Truly I tell you, if you have faith as small as a mustard seed, you can say to this mountain, 'Move from here to there,' and it will move. Nothing will be impossible for you."

For quite some time, Frank was adamant that that nobody was to know about his condition. In the past he has shared many personal matters with friends, online, and in his prior books. Deep down, I always felt that the day would come when he was ready to share this journey, too. When that might happen, or how, I had no idea. So I was not surprised when he did write this book, only that he was ready so soon. It quickly became clear that this time, he was truly pulling the curtain all the way back so he could help you.

Of course I'm a fan of all of Frank's previous books: the mindset/self-help, spiritual, young reader fantasy, philosophy, and real estate titles. Because in my experience, you will find the most useful information, advice, and understanding from somebody who has walked the talk. That is what Frank brings to the table, always. This book, while notably raw and revealing, also lays out a valuable, viable plan of action. I would have snapped *Adversitology* up in a second if it had been available way back when I was taking care of my mom, because it contains information that could be a true game-changer for all concerned.

When Frank's "condition" arrived, I was experienced at being a health advocate and not taking no for an answer. I personally had lived through this scenario before. What I knew deep down, from the moment we got the news, is that there is no such thing as impossible. That word does not belong in my vocabulary, nor does it belong in Frank's. It is with this mindset that I walked this path at Frank's side. It is with this outlook that I do my best to face every single day. I know firsthand what perseverance and faith can bring: miracles.

FRANK'S JOURNAL

(July 2022)

I sit here in our glass cabin surrounded by the most beautiful setting in our Mountain-Modern home. Allow yourself to breathe it in. Soak in the solitude: the sound of the stream, all the beautiful trees and foliage rustling, the buzzing of flying things, the warmth of the sun on my face, the sound of birds chirping . . . these are all love.

Another year older, and I am wiser. Put that wisdom to good use! The cycle can be, and has been, broken. But not through willpower, or quitting anything cold turkey, but by being aware of the existence of the cycles in the first place.

A cycle will only take you around in circles, repeating behavior ingrained through attachments that were only broken when a new attachment took its place.

The glass cabin along the Pigeon River in Canton, North Carolina

See people and familiar situations, like Nilsa, in a whole new light. You ceased looking for her inherent beauty a long time ago. Stop and see her again for the first time. Do the same thing with Laura. With your mom. With all those you have known for a long time.

A cycle will only take you around in circles, repeating behavior ingrained through attachments that were only broken when a new attachment took its place.

As for anyone you don't like, see the conditioning in yourself from your upbringing that causes you to see them in this way.

Finally, be kind to your body. It has gone through so much, and yes, it is slowly, irreparably breaking down as God and nature intended.

Most important of all, be kind to your mind. Be aware of the things that you are, and the things that you are not. This is your life. Why not you, Frank?

———⊃«O»⊂———

Y NOT YOU
(YOUR FINAL ASSIGNMENT!)

For your final *Adversitology* action item, let's answer the question posed by the title to this chapter, Y (Why) Not You? As you read *Adversitology* there were turning points for you, breakthroughs in how to see and approach your adversity or adversities, current or future.

List three major turning points, big breakthroughs, or significant revelations you experienced reading this book that will help you (and others) answer the question, *Why not you?* (If you'd like to share them with others, head over to Adversitology.com or post and use #Adversitology.)

1) _____

_____

_____

_____

2) _____

_____

_____

_____

3) _____

_____

_____

_____

Thank you so much for sharing in this journey with Nilsa, Laura, and me (Frank). I love you.

MY DREAM

Which I had before I even started writing Adversitology

I am on one of my solo adventures and lost in the deepest, most remote part of the Amazon rain forest. I am starving, severely dehydrated, and badly injured from numerous falls caused by the dense flora and huge tree roots that serpentine across the rain forest floor. After weeks of struggling to find my way out, hope fades to desperation and then to resignation. I am only hours away from succumbing to imminent death.

Sitting slouched against the trunk of a large acai palm, with my last bit of energy, I look around and see a small, brightly colored leaf resembling a passionflower that is brilliantly illuminated by a single ray of sunlight penetrating the thick canopy above. In my desperate, delusional, almost hallucinogenic state, the ethereal leaf appears to be beckoning me, so I lean over and pick it and, with a sense of surrender, I decide to eat it and a few more from that same plant.

My hunger, thirst, and pain miraculously vanish, and, stuffing a few magic leaves in my torn pants, I find the strength and will to make my way out of the rain forest and back to my family.

It turns out that these leaves came from a powerful, previously undiscovered native plant with miraculous healing properties. Years later, this plant is identified and used by pharmaceutical companies all over the world as an amazing breakthrough for those struggling with physical and emotional adversities.

EPIC EPILOGUE

FRANK'S JOURNAL

(October 2022)

I just re-read my journal entry from three months ago. That's right, less than three months ago I was walking on air, head in the heavens after a year-plus of perfect 0.000 percent readings. I was completely cured.

And now, I'm not. Just like that. The great mystery of life presents another chapter. One that has seen my PCR test for my all-important BCR/ABL numbers shockingly rise for the first time in 16 months. After all the prayers, Rosaries, journal entries, medication, suffering, etc., I'm served with this brutal subpoena. How can this be?!

What I really want to know in this frozen-in-time moment: How is it that I was feeling so good, so healthy, so happy just a few months ago, and now this? Is this God getting my attention for taking the gift of health he had given me for granted?

God, did something I do cause it to be snatched away? What do I need to do to have you bless me with health again? Or will you just wake me from what must be a bad dream?

———◉———

Can you fucking believe it? (Yes, it's me, talking "Frankly" to you in the first person. For this news, no more of me writing as if I'm a narrator or someone else. And yes, I cursed for the first time in this book.)

Talk about a punch to the gut on an ordinary Sunday afternoon, a few days after my routine, every-six-weeks checkup. This was one helluva jolt for the "new" me, and my immediate raging meltdown was anything but enlightened. Everyone vents differently, and I tend to do it violently. Nilsa was out of town, so I called her, broke the news, and hung up abruptly. Then there was a lot of cursing, questioning God, and vowing never to take that awful medicine again.

The rage passed quickly. And then it was a rapid descent into overwhelming despair, me curling up into a pathetic ball of tears, sinking into the couch like the witch melting into the floor in *The Wizard of Oz*. All those prayers, rosaries, journaling. All those painfully revealing words written in the hope of helping others.

And then it was a rapid descent into overwhelming despair, me curling up into a pathetic ball of tears, sinking into the couch like the witch melting into the floor in *The Wizard of Oz*.

After all I have read, studied, endured, and practiced to put multiple nails into the coffin of my adversity . . . and there, in an instant, all those nails were yanked out, turning what I thought was dead into a freaking zombie. It was back, stretching its ugly arms in my direction. Again!

Though truth to be told, I had a feeling that something was slightly off. I hadn't been feeling quite well in the weeks before this report. I was pushing my body way too hard with the running, keeping myself going with endless cortisone shots, anti-inflammatory medications, and steroids in a bid to keep myself out on the road, training for my next race.

After all I have read, studied, endured, and practiced to put multiple nails into the coffin of my adversity . . . and there, in an instant, all those nails were yanked out, turning what I thought was dead into a freaking zombie.

Was it possible that this monomaniacal training triggered the relapse? And there was something else. For months I had taken my 100 percent cure 100 percent for granted. I was no longer grateful for the gift of recovery. I had started to edge toward all the things that got me into trouble before, mainly these insane efforts to keep running when my knees are nearly shot. There was the stress of making two movies about choosing to unretire and come back to creating real estate artistry. On top of writing the scripts and filming the movies, I chose to have both premiere on the big screen at an IPIC theater in a short span of only seven months from concept to completion. There's also the fact that I discontinued my medication three months ago and considered myself done. After all, 16 months with 0.000 percent readings and I saw no reason to still need to push those pills through my lips. Makes sense, right? While Dr. Garcia had reluctantly agreed to my request to come off the medication, he would have preferred I stay on a small dose for another year at least.

True, the rise in numbers was very small, from quadruple-zero to 0.010. On the phone, Dr. Garcia was not overly concerned, as such fluctuations are not unusual.

"Frank, I don't want you to become upset. You're coming back in to see me in a couple of weeks. The trend overall has been very positive. Why don't we leave things as they are and just retest then?"

"Doc, I love you, but for 16 months it was all zeroes, all the time. This trend is now going in the wrong direction, up, and that's not positive. It's alarming! There's only one way to fix that. I am going to restart the medicine. I'm going back on it today!"

* * *

How I hate that medicine: the nausea, the hair loss, the loss of energy on high doses. But most of all, the pills remind me that I have an intruder in my body. But it's simply common sense, to me anyway, that if you want to reverse the trend and bring the numbers down, you do what corrected the numbers in the first place. Among other things, I resumed taking my medicine and jumped back in by taking 20 mg doses daily.

A sudden doubt hit me: *Should I consider shelving this book? Should I even release it? Will I have to toss months of work down the drain, because what I have written might not have worked?* I was sinking even lower. My "victory" suddenly felt hollow.

Here it comes, I thought, *the emotional collapse that I thought I'd never experience again.* In that moment, I felt the darkest depression I had known since my world upended with the original diagnosis two-and-a-half years before.

I had planned to have a regularly scheduled call with my collaborator, Julie, the very next day. So I was brooding about how to tell her that the 50,000+ words I had written, and she had labored over, might be headed straight for the top shelf in the back of the dusty storage closet.

But anger and self-pity both evaporated that morning. I had awakened to seeing this setback as an opportunity. *If I really believe in what I wrote, then this is simply one more of life's adversities.* It's something I warn readers will most definitely come during the normal course of life. Usually, it's something completely different, but in my case, whoops, exact same issue, second verse, same as the first. Ten minutes before I received the last report, I had been convinced this program not only helped me immensely but would help others. Why in the world would I abandon it? I resolved to go back to the well to give it a real test. It was time to put on my big-boy pants and revisit each letter, A-D-V-E-R-S-I-T-Y!

So it was less than 24 hours after getting the news when I called Julie for our weekly book conversation. I waited until the end to casually tell her the latest. She was unhappy and concerned for me when she heard this, of course, but she was mainly shocked that I sounded so calm and upbeat. It wasn't a show, though. I was calm and committed.

Instead of being a prescriber, I was a patient once again, and I was going to follow my own prescription. After all, if it worked once, I knew it would work again.

Over the next few months, I reapplied my own A-D-V-E-R-S-I-T-Y plan. I was glad I had it to lean on because the news was not encouraging. The results from my next reading a month later showed that my numbers were up even further, to 0.029. From 0.000 to 0.029 was not a hiccup, or an issue with the lab work. It was a significant rise in numbers two months in a row. This was simply a fact. I was on the wrong track, one that could spell a whole lot of physical, emotional, and spiritual pain again, maybe even ultimately lead to my death.

Instead of being a prescriber, I was a patient once again, and I was going to follow my own prescription. After all, if it worked once, I knew it would work again.

I was driving my 1990 Yugo a few days after the 0.029 reading, a straight shot of 14 hours all the way to our glass cabin in North Carolina. With no air conditioning, it was hot as hell. I ruminated, as hundreds of people plastered their cell phone cameras to the windows of their cars and took pictures while passing the guy in the beat-up, 0-60 in *never,* bankrupt Yugoslavian car. I pulled off to get gas for my 7-gallon tank (that means a fill-up every 300 miles or so). Bought an energy drink (which is rare for me), slammed it down, and had a small buzz going when I got back on the road and Dr. Garcia called. No doubt he wondered why I was talking so fast. With my escalating 0.029 mental shock still lingering, we had a conversation about upping the dose or not. He cautioned against going above 20 mg.

"Will I get back to straight zeroes if I take a higher dose, say 40 mg?" I asked him this question three times, three different ways, as he equivocated.

The third time I asked, Dr. Garcia got tired of this aggressive cross-examination. "Frank, you *may* get back there faster by taking a higher dose, but I am 100 percent sure you will eventually get back to quadruple zeroes."

Now, you *never* hear doctors make 100 percent guarantees like that. I knew I must trust this man. It was time to believe in this collaboration—again. I chose at that moment to believe that I would vanquish the rise in my numbers and get back to 0.000, and it would happen fast.

So what did I do (without telling him until later)? I compromised (if only with myself) and started taking 30 mg.

The next couple of months flew by as I eagerly accelerated all *Adversitology* had taught me (and hopefully you). Accept: easy. *This has happened, it's not a fluke, and I am living fully in this new reality.* Disidentifying was also a breeze. I refused to give this demon any power during the first go-round, and I wasn't about to do it on version 2.0. *I will not! After my brief meltdown, the collapse on the couch, the frantic call with the doctor, I am back to stubbornly refusing to let this intruder affect me!*

Of course I have already violated fate, many times, over the course of my treatment with Dr. Garcia. After the 0.010 reading, Dr. Garcia had told me not to worry and not start retaking the medication just yet, as the numbers would self-correct. I had gone back on the 20 mg dose that night, as I was not about to play wait and see. And after the 0.029 reading? I wanted to go to 40 mg, but I compromised (after hanging up with him) and went to 30 mg. I trusted Dr. Garcia implicitly, but those were my numbers heading north! My life. My call.

After the initial shock and cursing match with God, the hours-long slump into the couch springs, a mini-version of the meltdown from Round One, I immediately knew that once again I am not alone.

Then there's my strength: I stuck with the plan, every single day. Rigidly. I took it easy on the exercise and adherd to the healthiest lifestyle possible, and I took my maintenance-ish dose of medicine. In terms of risking it, this time around, I didn't have time to go there. It was premature to "reminisce" about a happy time when I was perfectly happy only months ago.

However, I will concede that I had taken a substantial risk in convincing Dr. Garcia to allow me to come off the medicine after 16 months of 0.000 readings. That decision has been AMA, as they say (against medical advice). Dr. Garcia was likely right in saying that I should have been on the maintenance dose for an additional year, and I had insisted (because I think I'm way smarter than I really am) that two years of medication was sufficient. You better believe I was in no hurry to come off it this time.

I savored everything over those couple of months. That feeling of taking recovery for granted? Over, done, out the window, this time forever. I have created weekly Priority Sheets for over 25 years, and health will *never* be missing from them again. Each sheet begins with the title MY LIFE written in large letters across the top, and commences every Monday. It has five categories: Personal/Family (the most important), Spiritual/Caring House Project (faith + sharing my blessings), Creative (real estate, books, art, movies) and Physical (exercise + heal). Under each category, I list my current goals and objectives. From that day forward, *never forget to be grateful for your health and for your life* will always be at the top of every single weekly list. (If you'd like to see my weekly priority sheet and adopt it for your use, visit Adversitology.com.)

It was never even a question: After the initial shock and cursing match with God, the hours-long slump into the couch springs, a mini-version of the meltdown from Round One, I immediately knew that once again I am not alone. I was never alone, not then and not now. My anger at God quickly turned to gratitude for the two years of health I enjoyed. *Please, don't leave me now (even if I may have upset you)*, I asked Him humbly from the start. After the momentary fit on the day of the shocking news, my faith was stronger than ever.

And so the weeks turned into months. Very soon it was time for my late December test. This time, I went in person to get my results. The verdict: 0.000, straight zeroes. I had faith this was going to happen. It was time to terminate, again. Except this time, I took my maintenance dose happily, easy as popping a baby aspirin every morning, and I heeded the goal in all caps on the top of my weekly Priority Sheets.

FRANK'S JOURNAL

(January 2, 2023)

I sit here on our deck high above the Pigeon River in Canton, North Carolina, the day after New Year's Day. A new year: 2023. The trees are bare. Winter is wafting through the frigid, crisp air. Looking at this barren landscape, one might be reminded of the starkness of death. But the cycle of life will soon start all over again in the spring.

Nature really doesn't suffer from adversity: it's a force, it's nature. But we humans do, and I did. Without *Adversitology's* saving grace, I would have likely suffered through this experience twice with the second being far worse than the first.

After 16 months of 0.000 readings, my numbers inexplicably began to rise. First, to 0.010, then to 0.029. Was my disease really back? Was all this reliving of the many ways I strived to overcome adversity for naught? Should I simply shelve this entire manuscript? I wondered . . .

NO!

I immediately reimmersed myself into all I had written with such passion and purpose. I put into practice, once again, all that I had just finished writing. I'm proud that I believed that the plan would work, and my numbers would return to all zeroes—and they did—very quickly.

I have learned my lesson well about taking my own prescription. The A-D-V-E-R-S-I-T-Y plan has come through for me, just as it did before!

As I sit here a few months after that slight hiccup, it's time to terminate once again. Why not you, Frank? Your numbers are officially back to 0.000. Congratulations, first you earned your master's, and now you have graduated to your own Ph.D. in *Adversitology.*

Do you remember that brightly colored, magical leaf from the tree in the Amazonian jungle from my dream at the end of Chapter 9? The one with the incredible healing properties that saved my life?

Leaves don't grow in isolation, you know. They are found on branches or vines surrounded by many other leaves. I found my magic leaf in a dream and translated it into my reality—and yours, too, I hope. I am now comforted and confident that there are plenty of others on that tree, waiting to help you overcome your life's adversities. Pluck yours, and in short order *Adversitology* will work its magic on you. I promise (x2).

We made it!

ACKNOWLEDGEMENTS

It's still me, Frank, in the first person. It wasn't easy to write most of this book in third-person as a narrator, then toggle between first-person journal entries and first-person accounts written by my wife, Nilsa, and daughter, Laura, and then, finally, finish the Epic Epilogue in first person. How did I do it and make it flow so well (I hope)? It wasn't "I" at all; it was us. I give full credit to my collaborator, Julie McCarron, for helping me tell this story using an incredibly unique, unproven writing approach. Everything we've done in writing *Adversitology* is so far outside publishing tradition that we've likely created a new one! Julie was on this thrill ride for over a year. She was the first person I relived *all* the details with. Not only was she my collaborator, but she was also part therapist, as I often got very emotional while re-creating this adversity for the first time with spoken and written words. Julie, thank you from the bottom of my heart.

What a joy it was to write *Adversitology* with contributions from Nilsa and Laura. I'm sure you looked forward to their stories in each chapter, and the impact my health adversity had on them. Often, it's the family and friends of those enduring an adversity who are overlooked as they endure a silent pain while their loved one suffers. As I was reading their stories, I learned a great deal from my two loves that I hadn't known before. I'm grateful that they took the time out of their busy schedules to write this book with me, as Nilsa runs her interior design business, and Laura runs her own company, StrataBrand. Besides writing the book with me, I am so blessed to have had them by my side as I overcame this health scare. It's not an overstatement to say I would have likely died without them. I love them both so much.

Speaking of dying, Dr. Eduardo Garcia saved my life. He is our angel. I imagine I'm not the easiest patient to care for. Everything you just read about me "negotiating" with him over treatment plans, medication dosages, exercise regimens, etc., was probably quite unusual for him to experience. I'm sure I created a form of adversity for him that he'll never forget! But there he was (and still is), using the most loving and sensitive approach I've ever witnessed in a doctor. I love you, Dr. G!

I mentioned there were only five people outside of my doctors and Julie who I chose to share my condition with. These five people represent that small inner circle that, when you look at the cover of this book and see the lifeline represented by the rope, served as just that, my lifeline over the past three years. In addition to Nilsa and Laura, I chose to share my diagnosis with my mom, Katie McKinney. Although I avoid burdening her with most all of my adversities, this one needed the love only a mother could give. She was strong and present, just like she has been for her other five children. I love you, Mom. I needed a spiritual advisor with a special anointing that I could lean on when I was scared or was struggling with my own faith. Juan Restrepo has been that person for the last 15 years. Juan's direct line to heaven and his full faith in God to restore me to health never wavered. The power of Juan's "1-800-Sav-Frnk" hotline and the faith he continues to share is otherworldly and heaven-sent.

Finally, let's face it, I'm pretty mercurial, intense, complicated, multidimensional, and, quite honestly, fucked-up at times. Imagine being my therapist! While I feel as though I've worn her out over the last decade, Dr. Jan Ganesh has cared for my mind when Sigmund Freud's ghost would have run for the hills. "Get the mind right and the _____ (money, miles, health, etc.) will follow" is something I shared in *Aspire!* and now share in detail at my keynotes. Dr. Jan did just that when my diagnosis was on the verge of causing complete emotional collapse.

A few months after the onset of my special condition I needed a place to get away to, an escape from the spotlight of South Florida where I could finish writing my book, *Aspire!* My best friend Steve Cruz and his wife, Diana, were kind enough to offer me the use of their cozy cabin in Canton, North Carolina, *anytime* Nilsa or I needed a quiet place. This serene setting in the mist-covered Blue Ridge Mountains helped bring me back to health and, eventually, led me to "unretire" and begin creating real estate artistry again. Thanks, brochacho!

Over the last 15 years I've had the good fortune of working with one of the few living superheroes I've ever met. In capacities too numerous to list, Karen Risch Mott has helped me with all my prior books dating back to *Make it BIG!, Frank McKinney's Maverick Approach; Burst This!; The Tap; Dead Fred, Flying Lunchboxes and the Good Luck Circle; The Other Thief;* and *Aspire!* She's organized multiple book tours and even crewed for me at one of my Badwater 135-mile ultramarathon races! Karen's contribution to *Adversitology* through copyediting and helping me publish it and record it for Audible under our own imprint (Caring House Books), is unduplicatable and sooooo appreciated.

Is it *Acknowledgements* or *Acknowledgments?* The importance of a proofreader to a book is akin to the significance of Clarence Jones to Martin Luther King, Jr.'s "I Have a Dream" speech, Benjamin Franklin to Thomas Jefferson's first draft of the Declaration of Independence, or Jay Ward for deciding to animate Cap'n Crunch's eyebrows *on* his hat instead of on his forehead. Without the unsung hero I found in Christine Van Zandt of Write for Success, and her proofreading ability, *Adversitology* would not have impacted you the way it was intend. (I mean *intended.*)

Take a look at that book cover! The artistic collaboration with designer and graphic artist Erik Hollander is something I always look forward to. Here's a little secret: When I start writing a book I always design the cover *first,* before I write word one. My book covers are conceived before I even write the chapter outline! That's because I want to deliver not only on the promise of the title but live up to the promise made by the cover image. As I write, I always have an image of the cover close by that I look at often for inspiration. Thank you, Erik, for this beautiful cover and the covers of four of my other books.

The interior design of a book is very much like the interior design of one of our oceanfront mansions. If it's not done properly with meticulous attention to detail, all you really have is a shell, and in the case of a book, just a bunch of black letters on white paper. When I decided to use this unique approach of toggling between third person, first person journal, and first-person contributors (Nilsa and Laura), the font styles, sizes, spacing, color gradient, chapter starts, page breaks, interior images layout. Yes, even that

Library of Congress copyright page helps make *Adversitology* very much like watching a movie without the screen. You can thank Robert Mott for the visual appeal of the interior of the book you hold in your hands.

Remember reading that there are approximately 2,350 new books published each day? Well, to sell books you need more than a captivating and evocative story. Within the four corners of a book is a small business that all authors hope turns into a big business. That doesn't happen on its own. There were many promotional pieces and beautiful color graphics created for *Adversitology* that told the book's story via social media, traditional media, e-mail blasts, etc. Brian Kay is the wizard behind the design of it all.

Let's stay with how a book is promoted for a second. Having the right publicist who knows how to accentuate you, your story, and your book, and make it all stand out from the rest is one of the most challenging parts of releasing a book. I started working with the team at Carli Brinkman Public Relations (and Carli herself) five months before the book was released. If you know me, you know I know a thing or two about publicity. Well, Carli knows a thing or *two hundred* about publicity and public relations. I *loved* working with her on this book, and when *Adversitology* hits the bestseller lists it will be due to the brilliance of Carli.

As of the writing of these acknowledgements, I have yet to settle on a theme for our book launch party. We're well-known for our dramatic, immersive, captivating, and theatrical unveilings and book launch events. If you were there or saw the March 11 launch event on social or Adversitology. com, it was Renee Radabaugh and her team at Paragon Events who helped create such a memorable and jaw-dropping spectacle.

Soon after *Adversitology* is released, I'll depart on "Frank McKinney's *Adversitology* Book Tour." The month-long odyssey will stop at 25 cities up and down the east coast and visit dozens of homeless shelters, soup kitchens, food pantries, veteran's facilities, abused women's shelters, juvenile detention centers, schools, hospitals, TV stations, radio stations, podcasts, and bookstores to deliver the message found in *Adversitology*. That tour wouldn't be possible without Juan Restrepo, whom I mentioned above. In addition to being my spiritual advisor, Juan is a 20-year Caring

House Project Board of Directors member who has driven the tour buses and provided the digital media for my book tours dating back to *The Tap* over a decade ago. Imagine being cooped up with me for 10,000 miles! Staying with the *Adversitology* Book Tour, I want to sincerely thank Dennis Moran, who is also a 20-year Caring House Project Board member, for scheduling all stops on the tour.

And finally, I give all glory and thanks to God for bringing me back to health and, through the Holy Spirit, encouraging me to write *Adversitology* and share its message with you. None of the preceding 50,000+ words, and all the ups and downs you and I both experienced, would have happened without that single word: *God*.

ABOUT FRANK McKINNEY

Frank McKinney is a true modern-day Renaissance man who has pushed the limits of success in his every endeavor. His early years were not very promising, however: upon attending his fourth high school in four years, as he was asked to leave the first three, he earned his high school diploma with a 1.8 GPA. (It would have been lower, but he received an A in creative writing.) So, with $50 in his pocket and without the benefit of further education, Frank left his native Indiana for Florida in search of his highest calling.

Today, Frank's life is a testament to the power of adversitology, aspiration, and the ability to overcome any obstacle to create a completely new reality. As a real estate artist, he has created and sold 44 oceanfront mansions on speculation, with an average price of $14 million. As a philanthro-capitalist, he has built 30 self-sustaining villages in Haiti over the last 20 years, providing more than 13,600 children and their families with homes, renewable food, and clean water, and the means to support themselves. A bestselling author, actor, and keynote speaker, he has written 8 books in 7 genres, starred in 4 movies, and keynoted before audiences of 10 to 10,000 around the world. Physically, Frank has pushed the limits of his body by racing in the Badwater 135-mile ultramarathon 12 times in the scorching summer in Death Valley, California, a race referred to by *National Geographic* as "the world's toughest footrace."

Frank believes you need a unique space or place to draw out creativity and ingenuity. He wrote the first half of *Adversitology* in his Delray Beach, Florida, oceanfront tree house office that has spectacular views and includes a bamboo desk, shower, bathroom, sink, air conditioning, hardwood floors, cedar walls, a loft with a king-size bed, and a suspension bridge to the master bedroom in the main house that's Frank's commute to and from work! He completed the second half of this book in his glass cabin along the Pigeon River in Canton, North Carolina. The commute there? It's up a whopping 72 steps ascending to what Frank refers to as his "stairway to writer's heaven."

Today, Frank and his wife, Nilsa, split their time between their home in South Florida and their glass cabin in the sky, along the river! They enjoy visiting their daughter, Laura, in New York City, where she started and runs StrataBrand, a brand strategy firm.

Share the Profound Message of

ADVERSITOLOGY

Give copies of *Adversitology* to family, friends and co-workers ...

Paperback (Caring House Books, 2023)
Available at Adversitology.com • $24.95

OTHER BESTSELLING OFFERINGS from Frank McKinney

Aspire! How to Create Your Own Reality and Alter Your DNA asks, "Can you really create your own reality and alter your DNA?" Real estate artist and 8-time bestselling author Frank McKinney has done just that. He's pushed the limits professionally (creating then selling 44 multimillion-dollar oceanfront mansions on spec), philanthropically (building 30 self-sustaining villages in the poorest country on earth), creatively (writing 8 books in 7 genres), and physically (running the Badwater 135-mile ultramarathon 12 times).

Paperback, hardcover, Audible, Kindle, and autographed (Caring House Books, 2021) • Available at TheAspireBook.com • $30.00

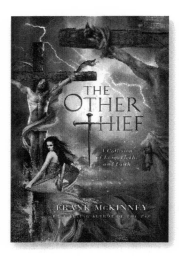

The Other Thief is a controversial, heart-wrenching novel of deception, pride, and lust, along with mercy, grace, forgiveness, and—above all—love. Frank McKinney boldly enters the Christian romance genre with this seductively spiritual novel. *The Other Thief* will arouse readers and their faith, leaving them wondering which side of the cross they would choose.

Hardcover (HCI, 2018)
Available at TheOtherThief.com • $20

Bestselling author Frank McKinney introduces *The Tap,* a profound spiritual practice leading to success in the business of life. Your prayers for more are answered! *The Tap* shows how to sensitize yourself to feel and then act on life's great "Tap Moments," embracing the rewards and responsibilities of a blessed life. Feel it, follow it, and find your highest calling. This book is about accepting responsibility, and it gives you confidence in your ability to handle your "more," whether it's more wealth, health, happiness, or relationships.

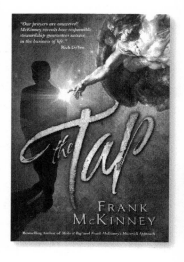

Hardcover (HCI, 2009) • Available at The-Tap.com • $25

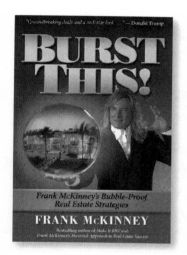

Burst This! Frank McKinney's Bubble-Proof Real Estate Strategies continues Frank McKinney's international bestselling tradition of delivering paradoxical perspectives and strategies for generational success in real estate. Tired of all the "bubble" talk, all the doom and gloom? Here comes McKinney in his unassailable fear-removal gear to help you wash away the worry—the anxiety that financial theorists and misguided media constantly dump into the real estate marketplace.

During his 30-year career, this "maverick daredevil real estate artist" has not only survived but thrived through all economic conditions by taking the contrarian position and making his own real estate markets.

Hardcover (HCI, 2009) • Available at Burst-This.com • $30

With ***Dead Fred, Flying Lunchboxes and the Good Luck Circle,*** Frank McKinney boldly enters young reader fiction with this middle-grade fantasy novel charged with fairy-tale wonder, enthralling magic, page-turning suspense, and the deep creativity he's known for. It will both race and gladden the hearts of readers of all ages. This classic was inspired by real-life Laura McKinney's 1,652 walks to school with her friends and her father, Frank McKinney.

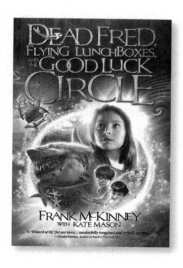

Hardcover (HCI, 2009)
Available at Dead-Fred.com • $25

Frank McKinney's Maverick Approach to Real Estate Success takes the reader on a fascinating real estate odyssey that began more than three decades ago with a $50,000 fixer-upper and culminates in $100 million mansion. Includes strategies and insights from a true real estate "artist," visionary, and market maker

Paperback (John Wiley & Sons, 2006)
Available at Frank-McKinney.com • $25

Make it Big! 49 Secrets for Building a Life of Extreme Success, Frank's first book, consists of 49 short, dynamic chapters that share how to live a life full of meaning and purpose, with real estate stories and "deal points" sprinkled throughout.

Hardcover (John Wiley & Sons, 2002)
Available at Frank-McKinney.com • $30

The Frank McKinney "Adversitology" Experience, Keynotes, Appearances, Personal "Aspire & Adversitology" Coaching
One-on-one or group events and bulk pricing.
Inquire: Pamela@Frank-McKinney.com

Please visit Frank-McKinney.com, which has been referred to as "Disney on a Desktop" by *PCMag,* for all things Frank McKinney! It's important to note that proceeds from the sale of *Adversitology* and all of Frank's books benefit his Caring House Project Foundation (CHPF). To learn more about CHPF and its 30 self-sustaining villages built in Haiti over the last 20 years, providing more than 13,600 children and their families with homes, renewable food, clean water, and the means to support themselves, visit CHPF.org.

 frank.mckinney.10

 frankmckinney

 thefrankmckinney

 frankmckinney

 frankmckinneyauthor

 frank-mckinney.com